TGIF

BUT WHAT WILL
I DO ON MONDAY?

SUSAN L. FISTER AND KAREN A. KEMP

TGIF: But What Will I Do on Monday? Trademarks

Popsicle® is a trademark of Gold Bond-Good Humor Ice Cream.
Transformer Pen® is a trademark of Pentech International, Inc.

08   07   06   05   12   11   10   9

Illustrations and cover art by Londerville Design

ISBN 1-57035-039-6

Printed in the United States of America

Published and Distributed by

SOPRIS
WEST™
EDUCATIONAL SERVICES

A Cambium Learning™ Company

4093 Specialty Place • Longmont, CO 80504 • (303) 651-2829
www.sopriswest.com

61TG/9-05

About the Authors

Susan L. Fister is currently working as an inservice educational presenter/consultant and staff developer for many school districts throughout the country. Susan is involved in helping school staff include challenging students into classroom programs. She conducts workshops on inclusion, collaboration, and co-teaching. She also reinforces the "nuts and bolts" of validated instructional strategies, behavior management, social skills, and the monitoring of student progress. Susan also has a contract with the Utah State Office of Education to assist with statewide personnel development and school-based training of educational teams involving behavioral and educational strategies. She has over 25 years of educational experience in the field as a teacher, clinical instructor, supervisor, staff developer, classroom-based researcher, and project coordinator for the Utah Learning Resource Center. Susan is an adjunct faculty member at both Utah State University and the University of Utah and has published numerous journal articles, book chapters, video tapes, instructional materials, and technical assistance papers for teachers.

Karen A. Kemp is currently working as Director of Special Programs in the Cahoes City School District of New York. She is also an inservice educational presenter/consultant and staff developer for school districts throughout the country. Karen is involved in training school personnel to effectively accommodate challenging students into classroom programs. She provides training in the areas of strategy instruction, IEP development, reading, coteaching, building-based support teams, and social development. Karen has over 15 years in direct teaching experience with students who have mild to severe disabilities, as well as general education classroom teaching. She also served as a program specialist for a statewide staff development project and participated for four years in a research translation and implementation grant. Karen holds an administrative credential, and has published numerous journal articles, book chapters, video tapes, and instructional materials.

Acknowledgments

We want to thank the many people who have helped bring this book into being. We are convinced that no book or important piece of work is ever the result of the efforts of just one person. This product reflects not only our own experiences in teaching, but contributions from many of the expert teachers, just like you, who are making efforts to improve the quality of classroom instruction for all students. We are especially grateful to our own children, Erica Ryberg, Corey Kemp, and Curtis Kemp, for their ideas and support while continuing to teach us about the important things in life. We also wish to thank Duane Webb and Stuart Horsfall at Sopris West for believing in us, and Ray Beck for introducing us to a range of opportunities.

We dedicate this book to all the students who have improved our teaching and the voices of wisdom who have whispered to us along the way. Some of those voices include:

Janet Freston
Utah State Office of Education
Salt Lake City, UT

Cyrus Freston
Ogden School District
Ogden, UT

Anita DeBoer
DeBoer-Haller Corporation
Chicago, IL

Denise Conrad
Great Falls Public Schools
Great Falls, MT

Candy Barela
Santa Ana Unified School District
Santa Ana, CA

Carol Massanari
Southeast Regional Resource Center
Lexington, KY

Phillip McLaughlin
University of Georgia
Athens, GA

Stephen J. Bavolek
Family Development Resources, Inc.
Park City, UT

Ken Reavis
Utah State Office of Education
Salt Lake City, UT

Tricia Wells
Mountain Plains Regional Resource Center
Des Moines, IA

Carol Hvidston
Sweetwater County School District
Rock Springs, WY

Ogden Lindsley
Educational Consultant
Lawrence, KS

Stevan Kukic
Utah State Office of Education
Salt Lake City, UT

Thomas Lovitt
University of Washington
Seattle, WA

Sigfried Engelmann
Engelmann-Becker Corporation
Eugene, OR

Michael Maloney
Quinte Learning Center
Bellville, Ontario, Canada

Randy Sprick
Educational Consultant
Eugene, OR

Kathy Pidek
Success by Design
Chicago, IL

Ken Howell
Western Washington State University
Bellingham, WA

Questions at a Glance

T1 What can I do about the students who do not achieve the classroom goals and objectives?

T2 What can I do about the students who do not respond to my instructions?

T3 What can I do about the students who do not participate during my instruction?

T4 What can I do about the students who disrupt during my instruction?

T5 What can I do about the students who forget information that I presented yesterday or a few hours ago?

T6 What can I do about the students who fail to see the relevance of my instruction?

T7 What can I do about the students who, following my instruction, do not understand or misgeneralize the concept?

T8 What can I do about the students who do not volunteer during my instruction?

T9 What can I do about the students who make hesitant responses or frequent errors during my instruction?

T10 What can I do about the students who have difficulty taking notes during my instruction?

T11 What can I do about the students who have a difficult time determining the critical information from my instruction?

T12 What can I do about the students who do not respond to my questions?

G1 What can I do about the students who do not begin or complete practice/seatwork activities?

G2 What can I do about the students who make careless errors when completing practice/seatwork activities?

G3 What can I do about the students who do not comprehend and/or respond to written material during practice/seatwork activities?

G4 What can I do about the students who do not work cooperatively, or rely on others to do the practice/seatwork activities?

G5 What can I do about the students who do not contribute to class discussions during practice activities?

I1 What can I do about the students who do not organize or manage assignments, materials, and/or time?

I2 What can I do about the students who do not complete or submit assignments?

I3 What can I do about the students who do not understand the independent assignment?

I4 What can I do about the students who do not check work for accuracy and/or completeness?

I5 What can I do about the students who do not know how to prepare and/or study for a test?

F1 What can I do about the students who do not perform well with traditional test formats?

F2 What can I do about the students who do not use strategies for taking a test?

F3 What can I do about the students who do not monitor work performance?

F4 What can I do about the students who do not respond to traditional grading procedures?

Table of Contents

[T1] What can I do about the students who do not achieve the classroom goals and objectives? 15

[T2] What can I do about the students who do not respond to my instructions? 21

---

* A blackline master of the form/material shown is available for reproduction in the companion book, *TGIF: Making It Work on Monday*.

---

* A blackline master of the form/material shown is available for reproduction in the companion book, *TGIF: Making It Work on Monday.*

T6 What can I do about the students who fail to see the relevance of
my instruction? 37

	NUMBER	TECHNIQUE	PAGE #
	1	Rationale Questions	37
	2	Think and Say Why	37
	3	Share Your Reasons	37
	4	What, Where/When, and Why	37 *
	5	Futures Map	38 *

T7 What can I do about the students who, following my instruction,
do not understand or misgeneralize the concept? 39

	NUMBER	TECHNIQUE	PAGE #
	1	Positive and Negative Examples	39
	2	Strategies and Rules	41
	3	Corrective Feedback	42
	4	Concept Angles	43
	5	Plus, Minus, Interesting (PMI)	43
	6	I Question That!	43
	7	Know/Want to Know/Learned (KWL)	44
	8	Learning Logs	44 *
	9	Study Guides (Margins)	45
	10	Graphic Organizers (Sequence)	45
	11	Attribute Maps	46

T8 What can I do about the students who do not volunteer during my
instruction? 47

	NUMBER	TECHNIQUE	PAGE #
	1	Group/Individual Questioning	47
	2	Responses Without Talking	47
	3	I am Ready	47
	4	Please Come Back	48
	5	Name's Up Volunteer Board	48
	6	Heads Together	48
	7	Folded Corners	49
	8	Draw-a-Name	49

---

* A blackline master of the form/material shown is available for reproduction in the companion book, *TGIF: Making It Work on Monday.*

---

* A blackline master of the form/material shown is available for reproduction in the companion book, *TGIF: Making It Work on Monday.*

---

* A blackline master of the form/material shown is available for reproduction in the companion book, *TGIF: Making It Work on Monday.*

---

* A blackline master of the form/material shown is available for reproduction in the companion book, *TGIF: Making It Work on Monday.*

* A blackline master of the form/material shown is available for reproduction in the companion book, *TGIF: Making It Work on Monday.*

Independent Practice Activities 107

* A blackline master of the form/material shown is available for reproduction in the companion book, *TGIF: Making It Work on Monday.*

* A blackline master of the form/material shown is available for reproduction in the companion book, *TGIF: Making It Work on Monday.*

---

* A blackline master of the form/material shown is available for reproduction in the companion book, *TGIF: Making It Work on Monday.*

---

* A blackline master of the form/material shown is available for reproduction in a companion book, *TGIF: Making It Work on Monday.*

Introduction

Why a Book on TGIF?

Today, it is not uncommon in our schools to see more students with challenging academic and social behaviors being included in less restrictive environments. This means that many students who had previously been served in self-contained classes or other special programs are now transitioning to neighborhood schools and regular classroom settings. Consequently, educators who have not been trained in procedures for modifying and adapting instruction are facing a greater number of challenges in terms of accommodating a more diverse group of students. Furthermore, recent legislation has made it necessary for educators to implement **reasonable accommodations** in the regular classroom setting as a first step in meeting the needs of **all** students. Additional resources are required in order to accommodate the increasing range of student needs.

This book is designed as one such resource to give educators options and ideas for accommodating students throughout the instructional process. This book does not directly address **performance deficits.** Performance deficits are defined as situations where the student possesses the skill but chooses not to perform the skill. We view these problems as primarily motivational and behavior management issues. Where appropriate, motivational techniques are included. In addition, some ideas for reinforcing students with praise and tangible rewards like points or tickets are suggested.

The majority of the techniques contained in this book address instructional issues from the perspective of **skill deficits.** Skill deficits are defined as situations where the student does not possess the necessary skills to perform the task or behavior. The authors of this book believe that discrepancies in student performance should first be viewed as skill deficits or teaching opportunities. Hence, when a student is not performing, instructional strategies are recommended in the **teaching environment (T), the practice environment (G & I), or the measurement environment (F)**.

The instructional process has been divided into four components that educators address everyday (**T**: Teacher-Directed Instruction, **G**: Guided Practice Activities, **I**: Independent Practice Activities, **F**: Final Measurement). Each component represents a separate section of the book and includes a compilation of questions that we have been asked over the last fifteen years regarding students who were not encountering success in the classroom.

Who Can Use This Book?

This book is a collection of practical accommodations that can be integrated during the instructional process (TGIF). These ideas can be used with students who are not encountering success or those who are falling between the cracks within the existing instructional process. Unfortunately, this book does not offer all of the possible solutions to the myriad of instructional challenges that are faced in today's classrooms. It will hopefully trigger your own thinking and assist you to generate many more instructional techniques!

This book is designed to assist:

- Teachers who are working alone in a classroom setting

- Teachers who are collaborating with other staff
- Teacher assistance teams
- Related service providers (i.e., psychologists, diagnosticians, therapists, etc.)
- Special education personnel
- Paraprofessionals
- Parents
- Others who are looking for alternatives for dealing with instructional challenges

What is TGIF?

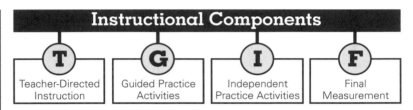

T: Teacher-Directed Instruction

Throughout **T**, the teacher orchestrates the teaching process by gaining attention, reviewing, covering goals and objectives, and discussing the rationale. The teacher presents new information, skills, and vocabulary. He or she models and demonstrates examples of new concepts, strategies, and rules, and asks appropriate questions to check for initial student understanding. High rates of active student involvement, fast-paced lessons, immediate positive feedback, and correction procedures for student errors are evident during the course of Teacher-Directed Instruction.

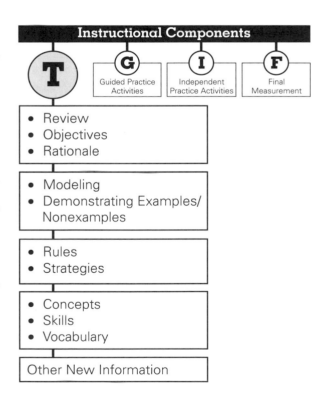

G: Guided Practice Activities

Throughout **G**, the teacher leads and prompts students through structured activities which are designed to provide frequent opportunities for students to practice new skills. Practice can be arranged individually, or through a variety of peer mediated structures like cooperative learning and classwide peer tutoring. These practice opportunities are directly related to the outcomes, and assist students in reducing errors as they are mastering new information. A suggested guideline for mastery after completing Guided Practice Activities involves high levels of accurate performance ranging from 85% to 95% correct. If students have not achieved high levels of mastery, then reteaching must occur, accompanied by additional appropriate practice activities. The consequences of not reteaching will result in unwarranted academic failure.

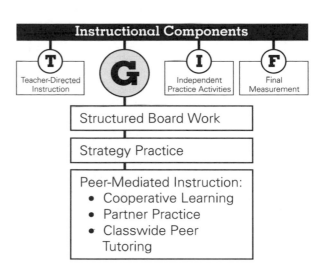

I: Independent Practice Activities

Throughout **I**, the teacher facilitates activities that provide continued or extended practice opportunities. These activities involve fewer prompts and less guidance from the teacher as students are now building fluency and generalizing the information related to the instructional outcomes. Successful completion of independent work involves continued high levels of accuracy as well as an appropriate speed of response. If students are not able to perform the skill independently, it may be necessary to provide more guided practice or teacher-directed instruction.

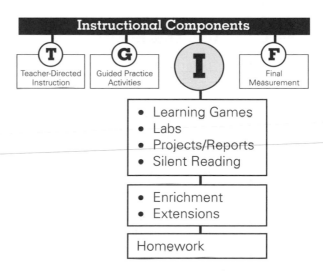

F: Final Measurement

F is defined as an end of unit measurement rather than the checking for understanding that occurs during the lesson. This type of measurement, which may be included in a student portfolio, is valued as an integral and legitimate component of the overall instructional process. Appropriate measurement can also serve as a powerful instructional tool. Throughout **F**, the teacher designs an end of unit performance assessment(s) that

adequately reflects the objectives identified in a unit of curriculum. The measurement instrument/tool is administered repeatedly (on the first day of instruction and as often as possible throughout the instructional unit) in order to determine if the students are progressing toward the end of unit objectives. In other words, one might think of the pretest and the posttest being administered as many times as possible throughout the unit. Without ongoing measurement, it is difficult to determine whether or not students' performance is improving, staying the same, or getting worse. Furthermore, powerful in-

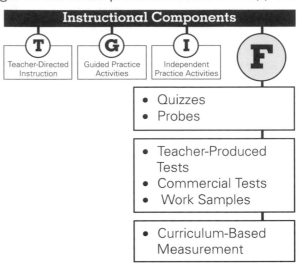

structional effects are lost. In order to effectively manage Final Measurement and insure immediate feedback to the learner, it is important that students learn to keep track of their own performance. Ongoing decisions can then be made regarding possible instructional changes that may be necessary throughout the **T**, **G**, **I**, and **F** process.

How Can I Use This Book?

1. Determine if you need an instructional accommodation for T, G, I, or F.

2. Refer to the table of contents and read through the questions.

3. Find a question that best represents the challenge you are facing.

4. Locate the section and page number for that question in the Table of Contents.

5. Read the suggested accommodations for that question and choose a technique that fits your situation. You can also modify, adapt, or create a new accommodation based on the ideas presented.

6. Refer to the Quick Reference Guide (page 167) for an alphabetical listing of all instructional ideas under each area of TGIF, with page numbers and implementation time codes.

The following codes have been provided to assist you in selecting and implementing the techniques.

"Zap!" can be implemented with little preparation time.

 "Hmm" requires a bit more preparation and time or materials, but well worth the effort!

 The **book icon** means that a full size illustration of the form/material is included in the separate companion book, *TGIF: Making It Work on Monday*. This book contains blackline masters which are ready to copy and use in the classroom.

How Long Should I Spend on Each Component of TGIF?

The circle graph below illustrates approximate percentages of time that could ideally be devoted to each of the instructional components. The time allotments should be viewed in terms of a daily lesson, weekly instruction, or a unit of instruction. In most instances, **Teacher-Directed Instruction** precedes **Guided** and **Independent Practice Activities**.

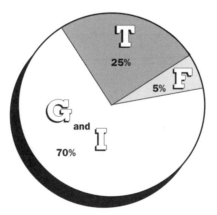

What Are Some Assumptions Underlying TGIF?

1. Schools, classrooms, and educational personnel are caring and nurturing. They treat students with dignity and respect, and promote the concept that all students belong in the least restrictive environment possible.

2. Fairness does not mean everyone gets the same treatment. Fairness means that everyone gets what he or she needs.

3. Appropriate outcomes/curriculum have been well articulated and communicated for all students.

4. Carefully planned lessons are used that incorporate validated elements of effective lesson design and delivery.

5. When students do not learn, they need to be retaught, **not blamed**, **ignored**, or **left to fall behind**.

How Can I Design Instruction According to TGIF?

Use the **TGIF Instructional Organizer** (example on page 6) as a planning tool for promoting effective instruction as well as a document to record accommodations that may be made during T, G, I, and F. The organizer can be used by an individual teacher, collaborating teachers, or grade level teams as they plan for instruction. The Organizer also lends itself well to planning for integrated and thematic units of instruction.

The Instructional Organizer defines components of effective instruction and includes some questions to consider as you develop lessons using TGIF. It is useful for planning daily instruction, weekly instruction, or longer units of instruction. Following the example organizer, a blank Instructional Organizer is included for duplication.

Instructional Organizer

(Page 1)

Unit: _____ Date: _____ Teacher(s): _____

Objective: _____ Subject/Period: _____

Teacher-Directed Instruction　　Who? _____ Time/Day: _____

G Gain Attention

Gain the attention of every student at the beginning and throughout instruction. Use the following procedure:
- Give a verbal or nonverbal prompt.
- Pause and wait for student compliance.
- Scan the classroom by visually scanning and physically moving around the room.
- Give feedback to the students by describing their appropriate behavior.

R Review

Active review, rather than passive, is conducted prior to, during, and after the introduction of new topics. Students are continuously recycling important information which relates to both the current and past topics. Active review can include asking content questions from previous lessons, asking questions related to the lesson objective and rationale, correcting homework, incorporating review questions from previous units on current tests, and cumulative review during a lesson. Active review involves eliciting high rates of group and individual responses.

O Objective

The lesson objective is clearly communicated in terms of what the student will be able to do as a result of the instruction, such as, "You will be able to write, list, compare, demonstrate, analyze, or critique." The verb that is used in the objective should match the level of cognition that is the focus of instruction and measurement. The objective is verified with students by asking a question such as, "What will you be able to do at the end of the lesson?" The objective is specific, measureable, and directly connected with the end-of-unit objectives, and the test or measurement that will be used to assess mastery.

W Why?/Rationale

The rationale for the lesson is clearly communicated in terms of how the mastery of the objective will benefit the student both in and out of the classroom. Examples are provided that are relevant to the learner and related to past and future instruction. The rationale is verified with students by directing questions and eliciting student responses that address the important benefits. For example: "It is important to be able to define the words so you can be understood when you communicate with other people and get your needs met."; or "It is important to be able to follow instructions and accept feedback so that you will get your work done the correct way. Your future boss will also view you as a good worker, and you'll have a better chance of getting a raise."

Instructional Organizer

(Page 2)

Teacher-Directed Instruction
(continued)

Who?_____   Time/Day:_____

I & Q Input and Questioning

Sequence:
"I Do It" (Modeling)
"We Do It" (Prompted)
"You Do It" (Unprompted)

Concepts, Skills, Vocabulary

Examples/Nonexamples

Rules/Strategies

Questions
Prompted
Unprompted

Explicit teacher modeling and multiple demonstrations of the new skill and/or concept is followed by teacher questions to check for comprehension. The questions are first directed to the examples which were modeled. If students are correct, then questions regarding similar examples that were not modeled are asked to determine if students can begin to generalize the information. The underlying format for this phase of instruction is "I Do It" (modeling), "We Do It" (prompted), and "You Do It" (unprompted). During this component, the teacher is overt not covert. The teacher articulates the process by using several pairs of examples and nonexamples. These examples represent a wide range and highlight the critical attributes of the concept. The teacher maintains a sequential and consistent presentation format. Questions to students following the model may require more or less teacher cues depending upon the student's responses. Eliciting frequent group responses during the prompted and unprompted questioning gives the teacher feedback regarding the need to reteach.

Instructional Organizer

(Page 3)

(*Please see pages 1-3 of this book for instructions on how to use this section.*)

Guided Practice   **Who?** _____ **Time/Day:** _____

☐ Content Practice ☐ Strategy Practice ☐ Structured Boardwork ☐ Peer-Mediated Instruction	Monitoring/ Feedback
Explanations/Directions to Students	

Independent Practice   **Who?** _____ **Time/Day:** _____

☐ In-Class ☐ Homework ☐ Extensions ☐ Out-of-Class	Monitoring/ Feedback
Explanations/Directions to Students	

Final Measurement   **Who?** _____ **Time/Day:** _____

☐ Quizzes ☐ Probes ☐ Curriculum-Based Assessment ☐ Portfolio ☐ Teacher-Produced Test	Monitoring/ Feedback
Explanations/Directions to Students *Procedures for:* ☐ Counting ☐ Recording ☐ Charting ☐ Timing Period	

Instructional Organizer

(Page 1)

Unit: _____ Date: _____ Teacher(s): _____

Objective: _____ Subject/Period: _____

Teacher-Directed Instruction   **Who?** _____   **Time/Day:** _____

G **Gain Attention**

R **Review**

O **Objective**

W **Why?/Rationale**

Instructional Organizer

(Page 2)

Teacher-Directed Instruction
(continued)

Who? _____   Time/Day: _____

I & Q Input and Questioning

Sequence:
 "I Do It" (Modeling)
 "We Do It" (Prompted)
 "You Do It" (Unprompted)

Concepts, Skills, Vocabulary

Examples/Nonexamples

Rules/Strategies

Questions
 Prompted
 Unprompted

Instructional Organizer

(Page 3)

Guided Practice   Who? _____   Time/Day: _____

☐ Content Practice   ☐ Strategy Practice

☐ Structured Boardwork   ☐ Peer-Mediated Instruction

Explanations/Directions to Students

Monitoring/ Feedback

Independent Practice   Who? _____   Time/Day: _____

☐ In-Class   ☐ Homework   ☐ Extensions

☐ Out-of-Class

Explanations/Directions to Students

Monitoring/ Feedback

Final Measurement   Who? _____   Time/Day: _____

☐ Quizzes   ☐ Probes   ☐ Curriculum-Based Assessment

☐ Portfolio   ☐ Teacher-Produced Test

Explanations/Directions to Students

Procedures for: ☐ Counting ☐ Recording ☐ Charting

☐ Timing Period

Monitoring/ Feedback

Teacher-Directed Instruction

1.1 Cognitive Shift

 Change the behavior expected of the students to another level in Bloom's Taxonomy using the chart on the following page. Choose a specific behavior from the chart that closely reflects what you want the student to achieve.

EXAMPLES

- An **application** level objective could be changed to a more simple **knowledge** level objective:

  Existing Objective: "Solve a word problem" in math

  Adapted Objective: "Identify key words" in word problems

- An **evaluation** level objective could be changed to a more simple **application** level objective:

  Existing Objective: "Critique the use of five social skills" used during a television interview

  Adapted Objective: "Demonstrate the steps of five social skills" observed during the interview

  ---

  Note: Use the Cognitive Processing Chart for lists of verbs/ behaviors that correspond to different levels of cognition.

Cognitive Processing Chart

MORE SIMPLE ←————— COGNITIVE PROCESSES —————→ MORE COMPLEX

Evaluation

appraise	measure
access	rank
critique	rate
determine	recommend
evaluate	select
grade	test
judge	

Synthesis

integrate	prescribe
organize	produce
plan	purpose
prepare	specify

Analysis

analyze	formulate
arrange	generalize
combine	group
construct	infer
create	order
design	separate
detect	summarize
develop	transform
explain	

Application

apply	illustrate
calculate	practice
classify	relate
complete	solve
demonstrate	use
employ	utilize
examine	

Comprehension

associate	distinguish
classify	estimate
compare	extrapolate
compute	interpret
contrast	interpolate
describe	predict
differentiate	translate
discuss	

Knowledge

count	recall
define	recite
draw	recognize
identify	record
indicate	repeat
list	say
match	state
name	tabulate
point	trace
quote	write
read	

T1: What can I do about the students who do not achieve the classroom goals and objectives?

1.2   Condition Shift

Narrow or broaden the amount of time, the setting, or the circumstances in which the student is to perform the desired behavior.

EXAMPLES

- **Reduce the duration of time for performance of the behavior.**

  Instead of expecting the student to follow instructions **throughout** a six-hour school day, the student could be expected to follow instructions during a 30-minute reading activity.

- **Change the circumstances in which the student is expected to demonstrate the behavior.**

  Instead of expecting the student to transition from one activity to another **independently**, the student could make the transitions with the **assistance** of a peer buddy.

1.3   Proficiency Shift

The following terms represent three hierarchical levels of proficiency:

- **Accuracy**

  The number of items correct.

- **Mastery**

  The number of items correct in a specified amount of time.

- **Automaticity**

  The number of items correct, in a specified amount of time with distractors present.

When modifying these levels, **automaticity** should be strongly considered for objectives that represent high priority or functional skills.

EXAMPLES

- An objective which requires **accuracy** might read, **Write/spell ten words 100% correctly**.

- An objective which requires **mastery** would involve performing the behavior accurately and quickly, such as, **Write/spell ten words correctly at a rate of 40 letters per minute in sequence**.

- An objective which requires **automaticity** involves completing the task accurately and quickly in the presence of relevant distractors. For instance, **write/spell words correctly in a 15-minute book report**.

T1: What can I do about the students who do not achieve the classroom goals and objectives?

1.4   Product Shift

Change the way in which the student is expected to demonstrate understanding of the concept.

EXAMPLE

If the outcome for the class is to indicate comprehension of a story topic by writing a book report, the target students could use alternate techniques to demonstrate the concept. Some alternative methods might include:

- An oral book report.

- Pictures to represent characters, setting, or events in the story.

- A play or skit.

- A story board.

- A collage.

1.5   Activity Change

Adapt or change the activities so target students can successfully participate in the class and complete the work.

EXAMPLES

- If the overriding class math objective is to solve computation problems and the target student is expected to **build skills**, the adapted activity could be:

  Use a calculator to complete the 20 problems with a partner.

- If the target student is expected to **demonstrate understanding** of the concept, the activity could be:

  Determine when to add and subtract numbers in a checkbook by marking a plus and minus sign in the margin.

- If the target student is expected to **increase participation** skills in the classroom, the activity could be:

  Make positive comments/gestures to peers in cooperative learning groups as other members of the group solve computation problems.

1.6   What Will I Do? Log

Provide the student with a log to record what they will be able to do as a result of the lesson. Communicate the objective in terms of what the student will be able to do at the end of the lesson.

Have students write the objective in their log exactly as you have stated

What Will I Do? Log

Name: _Benny_   Subject: _Language Arts_

TOPIC/ LESSON	DATE	OBJECTIVE
Punctuation	11/2	Write sentences correctly.

T1: What can I do about the students who do not achieve the classroom goals and objectives?

it or in their own words. Next, check for comprehension by having the students read aloud what they have written as a group, state the objective to each other, or show a partner what they have written in the log.

Add objectives to the log each time new information is presented. Have students keep the log in a notebook or folder to refer to throughout the lesson and the unit. Examples of effective objectives follow.

EXAMPLES

- "At the end of this lesson you will be able to pronounce and define five words."

- "You will be able to compare and contrast democracy and socialism."

- "You will be able to identify the problems that require regrouping."

Note: A similar strategy called *What, Where/When, and Why* found in T6.4 can be used for the same purpose.

1.7 Minimal/Advanced Competencies

Determine which skills are minimal competencies and which are advanced within the unit of instruction. Have students choose which objectives they will achieve based on teacher guidelines.

EXAMPLE

In a science unit on rocks and minerals, the following objectives would be presented in a competency contract to the students. Each objective is labeled with an (**m**) for **minimal** and an (**a**) for **advanced**.

- Define vocabulary (**m**)

- List three types of rocks (**m**)

- Identify the characteristics of each rock type (**m**)

- Translate the scientific rock and mineral names to common names (**a**)

Competency Contract

Unit: _Igneous Rocks_ Name: _Michael_ Date: _2/10_

Minimal Competencies	Advanced Competencies
I.D. Rock Names	Evaluate Neighborhood

- Compare and Contrast the three rock types (**m**)

- Evaluate the geographical area around your neighborhood and write a paper explaining your conclusions (**a**)

Note: All students are responsible for the minimal competencies and may choose which advanced competencies they would like to complete based on the teacher's guidelines.

T1: What can I do about the students who do not achieve the classroom goals and objectives?

2.1 Get Ready

Tell the students that a direction is about to be given. For example, say, "Get ready for an instruction," or switch a light globe on, or turn over a red card on the chalk board to signal the students that a direction is about to be given. If the students comply, reinforce them with a green card, a star next to their name, etc.

2.2 Listening Cues

Teach students that a particular sound or signal (i.e. a clapping rhythm, quiet hand raise, etc.) represents "eyes up here" or "stop, look, listen, and freeze." An electronic noise maker that produces a variety of different sounds can be used for this purpose. After giving the signal, pause, scan the classroom, and provide descriptive feedback to the students who are responding to the direction/signal. Frequent comments like "Good for Stuart, he stopped talking and looked at me when I gave the signal," should be given to students who respond to the signal.

2.3 You-Me Game

Set up a YOU-ME Chart on the chalk board. Each time the students use the predetermined steps (see T2.5) for following instructions, a point is quickly marked for the students under the **YOU** side. The teacher can say something like, "You got me!" If the students do not use the strategy for following instructions, the teacher quickly marks a point under the **ME** side of the chart. The teacher might say something like "I got you!" The daily counts under **YOU** and **ME** can also be recorded on a class chart that can serve as a challenge for the following day.

YOU	ME
///	/

2.4 I Can Say It

Ask the students to repeat the direction after it has been given to the class, or to an individual student. For example, "Raise your hand if you can repeat the instruction." Then, call on individual students or the entire class to repeat the instruction. After one student has repeated an instruction, call on another student to repeat what that student has just stated.

2.5   Following Instructions

Model each of the following steps for students. It is important to demonstrate several examples of what each of the behaviors/steps look and sound like. Also, demonstrate several examples of what each of the behaviors do not look or sound like.

Step 1: Look at the person giving the instruction when they say your name.

Step 2: Acknowledge that person after they have given you the instruction by saying, "yes," "okay," "alright," or another acceptable acknowledgement.

Step 3: Do the instruction immediately.

Step 4: Check back with the teacher if appropriate.

Each of the steps can be modified to fewer words, or pictures can be used to represent the steps. Rhymes or short phrases can also be used such as, **When given an instruction, look alive! Say "OK," and do it in five.**

A T-chart can be used, such as the one in the illustration below, to clarify for students what the appropriate behaviors look and sound like.

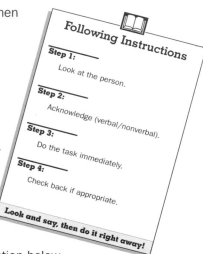

LOOKS LIKE	SOUNDS LIKE
In seat	No noises from hands, mouth, or body
Looking at person	No whining, pouting, or arguing while talking
Pleasant face	Saying "OK," "alright," or "yes"
Starting the task quickly	Pleasant voice

Source: Fister & Kemp, 1994.

2.6   Buddy Nose (Knows)

After the teacher has given the instruction, ask the students to tell the direction to the person sitting next to them. If correct, buddies (partners) award their dyad a point on their "buddy nose" card.

T2: What can I do about the students who do not respond to my instructions?

2.7   Behavior Bingo

When an individual student or the entire class follows an instruction, a square with a number written on it is drawn from an envelope. The numbered squares correspond with the numbers on the matrix; when the number is drawn its match is covered or crossed out on the matrix. When the student or the class achieve a bingo, a reward is given. The matrix cards can be 3x3, 4x4, or larger, depending upon the needs of the students, or the number of directions given in a 30-minute period.

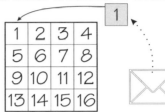

Source: Jenson, Rhode, & Reavis, 1994.

2.8   Yes/No Game

Make a stack of **Yes** and **No** cards, or slips of paper that are two different colors. When students comply with a direction, the teacher describes the behavior and places a **Yes** card into an opaque jar or bag. If a students do not comply with an instruction, then the teacher places a **No** card into the jar. If it is necessary to deliver a **No** card, the teacher's comments should be brief and business like, such as, "When I give an instruction, you need to look and do. A no card goes in the container." It is important to remember to use verbal praise and encouragement when the class earns **Yes** cards.

Students earn **Yes** cards or **No** cards continually throughout a class period based upon their ability to follow directions. At the end of the time period, the teacher pulls one card from the container. If it is a **Yes** card, the class earns a prearranged reward like minutes of free time, buddy time, or other privileges. If a **No** card is pulled then no reward is given.

Source: Jenson, 1994.

2.9   Tracking Directions

All students or a target student can be given a tracker card like the one in the illustration. The student is taught to circle a number (1) on the card when the teacher gives the first direction. The teacher should prompt students initially by saying something like, "Get ready for the first direction." The student circles the number and then decides if they followed the direction. If yes, the student puts a mark through the circled number. The card in the illustration shows that the student recorded the teacher giving nine instructions, eight of which the student followed during the recording period. It is useful for the teacher to keep a tracker card to determine the total number of instructions given. This also gives the teacher a way to check the students' accuracy at recording marks.

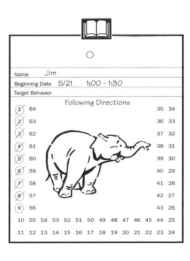

T2: What can I do about the students who do not respond to my instructions?

At the end of the marking period the student can count, record, and chart the number of corrects and errors which occurred or the percentage of directions followed. The students can punch a hole in the card each time a direction is followed. They can also paste their own photos on the card to personalize and add meaning to the procedure.

Source: Fister & Kemp, 1994.

T2: What can I do about the students who do not respond to my instructions?

3.1 Participation Board

Write student names in a column on a piece of poster board. This chart can be laminated for reuse. Place a mark next to the student's name each time an answer is given or information is volunteered related to the topic. Total the marks at the end of the time period and rein- force each student accordingly. Start over each day, each class period, or each content area.

Participation Board	
John S.	✓ ✓
Mary B.	✓ ✓
Lisa R.	✓
Curtis C.	✓ ✓ ✓

3.2 Participation Buddies

Allow the students to choose partners. After posing a question to the class, have everyone think about the answer individually, then turn to their assigned buddy and share the answer. The partners can then share the answer with the rest of the class.

3.3 Participation Jigsaw

Divide up the information and/or materials among the students so participation with others is necessary. Break students into groups of four. Each group is responsible for completing an assignment cooperatively. Give each student a part of the assignment to complete individually, then require each individual to share their information with the rest of the group. Make it clear to the students that every group member is accountable for all the information shared in the group. Group and/or individual tests can be administered after completion of the assignment.

Source: Johnson, Johnson, & Holubec, 1987.

3.4 Wild Card Spinner

The teacher and students should agree on a predetermined number of participation marks the students will try to earn during the class period. If the student earns the required number of marks, they are allowed a chance to spin. The rewards are listed on the Menu of Options, along with the unknown Wild Card. After using this procedure successfully, the teacher can vary the number of participation marks the students must earn, or have a mystery number that is written down and unknown to them. A chance to spin occurs if the students demonstrate the behavior at least the number of times written on the paper.

Step 1: The Spinner is divided into sections of various sizes and is numbered to correspond to the items on the Menu of Options. The number on each card represents a different positive reinforcer.

PIE CHART SPINNER

Step 2: The reinforcers are selected so that those of "higher" value (time, effort, money) correspond to the numbers in the smaller sections of the chart. Those of "lesser" value correspond to the numbers in the larger sections of the chart (see illustration). The section with the exclamation mark is the Wild Card and is unknown. The fact that this reinforcer is unknown adds an element of mystery and surprise to this technique. The Menu of Options is laminated so that the positive reinforcements can be changed periodically to maintain student interest and the effectiveness of the technique.

MENU OF OPTIONS

1. 1/2 homework
2. Floating "A"
3. Pencil
4. Spin tomorrow
5. One bonus point
6. Wild card

Step 3: The Wild Card reinforcer should be unique and of value to students. The unknown reinforcer is placed inside a large envelope or box, or the item name can be written on a slip of paper and placed inside an envelope. The envelope or box is then displayed in the prominent position in a classroom.

WILD CARD MYSTERY ENVELOPE

Step 4: When the student earns a reward, he or she receives a chance to spin the Wild Card Spinner, locates the corresponding number on the Menu of Options, and determines the reinforcement to be received.

Source: Adapted from Rhode, Jenson, & Reavis, 1993.

3.5   Participation Dots

Obtain a dot-to-dot picture from a coloring book or create a picture with dots arranged along the outside. Students track their participation by connecting the dots on the picture each time they participate in class. With each positive participation, the student is allowed to draw a line to the next dot on the picture. The student can earn rewards based on the number of dots connected during a specified period of time. The first or last dot of the day can be marked in order to visualize daily progress on the chart.

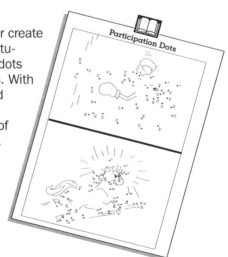

Source: Adapted from Rhode et al., 1993.

T3: What can I do about the students who do not participate during my instruction?

3.6   Mystery Motivators

The first component of Mystery Motivators is the reinforcer itself. The name of a reinforcer is written on a slip of paper and sealed inside an envelope. The second component is the chart on which the teacher has randomly marked reinforcement days with an **X**. Each day on the chart has a self-sticking dot on it. Each day or period the students have earned a reinforcement for positive participation, a dot is peeled off. If there is an **X** under the dot, the student is given the Mystery Motivator envelope to open. If there is no **X**, the student waits until the next day to earn a reinforcement and peel off another dot. Transformer Pens can be used instead of self-sticking dots to mark the **X**s on the chart.

Speed Away for a Mystery Motivator

Source: Rhode et al., 1993.

3.7   Participation Points

Provide students with a grading sheet that outlines the point system you have developed to reflect participation and effort during class. Establish the criteria for earning participation points by identifying the particular class behaviors that demonstrate excellence in participation.

EXAMPLES

Criteria for participation and effort (up to ten points can be earned per day/class):

- Bring pencil, paper, book, and other related materials (four points).

- Answer teacher-directed questions (one point each).

- Interact appropriately with other students during discussions (two points).

- Use target social behaviors such as, sitting up, eyes tracking teacher, getting teacher's attention with signal, accepting feedback, completing in-class assignments (two points).

Keep track of participation points using a recording sheet (see illustration). Record the number of points earned in the corresponding day of the week. Incorporate the points earned into the quarterly academic grade. Students can also monitor each other's participation using a similar recording sheet.

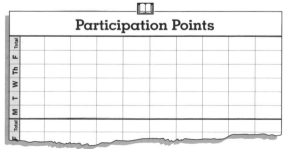

T3: What can I do about the students who do not participate during my instruction?

4.1   Everybody Say

Whenever you are giving information to the students, ask them to repeat it back to you or supply certain key words. By maintaining high rates of responses, students will be less likely to disrupt.

EXAMPLES

- "Sturdy means strong. Everybody, what does sturdy mean?"

- "Class, what is another word for strong?"

- "Here is a rule for regrouping. Whenever you take away more than you start with, you must regroup. Everybody, get ready to say the rule with me." Or, "Whenever you take away more then you start with, you must . . . " (students supply the missing word).

- "Everybody, what sound? what word?"

- "Class, spell the word aloud with me."

- "**Au** represents what element, everybody?"

- "Get ready to say the name of the main character. What is the name?"

- "Which family did Romeo belong to?"

4.2   Frequent Questions

Ask the disruptive students four times as many questions as you are currently asking during the problematic time period. These should be questions that you know the students can answer correctly.

Remember to first ask the question as if it were directed to the entire group ("Everybody, get ready to give me a definition for matter.") Pause for three to five seconds and then call on the target student. Call on the student when he or she is not disrupting and remember to follow the student's answer with descriptive praise.

T4: What can I do about the students who disrupt during my instruction?

4.3   On-Task Chart

A laminated chart or sheet of paper can serve as a visual display to post both the number of class disruptions and tasks completed during a specified time period. Students can be assigned to count the number in both categories. (The disruptive student can be given this responsibility!) Daily totals are charted on the bottom portion of the chart and a brief discussion with the students can follow to evaluate class performance. Reinforcement can be provided for achieving daily goals. You can also set goals for the next recording period.

On-Task Chart					Time Period: _____				
DISRUPTIONS *talk-outs*					**TASKS COMPLETED** *problems completed, answers, contributions*				
10	✔	✔			✔	✔	✔	✔	✔
9					✔	✔			
8									
7									
6									
5									
4									
3									
2									
1									
	Total: __2__					Total: __7__			

4.4   Name's-Up Listening Board

A Name's-Up Listening Board is a place where the teacher can quickly write/post students' names when they demonstrate good listening or attentive behavior. The board can be a portion of the chalkboard, a flip chart, a white board, etc. (see illustration below). When the teacher notices listening behaviors (e.g., looking at the teacher, attentive silence, quiet hand raises, relevant contributions, correct responses, etc.), the student's name is written on the Listening Board and the teacher verbally recognizes the behavior with an enthusiastic description of the behavior (e.g., "Wow, look at Susie. She is listening and giving quick answers!"). When students demonstrate continuing listening behaviors, the teacher can simply put asterisk or check marks (* or ✓) next to their name as the praise is delivered. At the end of the instructional period, the names can be erased and the activity repeated.

Listening Board	
James	✓ ✓ ✓
Karen	✓ ✓ ✓ ✓ ✓
Ray	✓
John	✓ ✓

4.5   Following Instructions

See T2.5 for information on applying the Following Instructions technique when dealing with disruptive students.

T4: What can I do about the students who disrupt during my instruction?

4.6   Keeping the Numbers Low

This is a classwide management system in which a limit for disruptions is predetermined for the entire class. Start with three cards of different colors or with the numbers 1, 2, and 3 written on them. The numbered cards indicate for the students the limits for disruptions. If a disruption occurs, the teacher turns over a card. If all cards are used, the class loses the reinforcer (which might be free time or some other privilege). When the number of disruptions decrease, the number of cards used can also decrease. This method can also be used with small groups of students or with an individual student where the cards are placed on the student's desk.

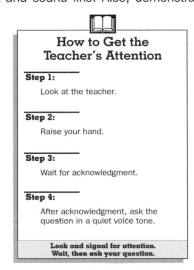

Source: Beck, 1993.

4.7   Getting the Teacher's Attention

Model each of the steps listed below for the students. It is important to demonstrate several examples of what each of the behaviors/steps look and sound like. Also, demonstrate several examples of what each of the behaviors do not look and sound like.

Step 1:   Look at the teacher.

Step 2:   Raise your hand.

Step 3:   Wait for acknowledgment.

Step 4:   After acknowledgment, ask the question in a quiet voice tone.

Each of the steps can be modified to fewer words or pictures can be used to represent the steps. Rhymes or short phrases can also be used such as, **Look and signal for attention. Wait, then ask your question.**

A T-chart can be used, such as the one in the illustration below, to clarify for students what the appropriate behaviors look and sound like.

How to Get the Teacher's Attention

Step 1:
Look at the teacher.

Step 2:
Raise your hand.

Step 3:
Wait for acknowledgment.

Step 4:
After acknowledgment, ask the question in a quiet voice tone.

Look and signal for attention. Wait, then ask your question.

LOOKS LIKE	SOUNDS LIKE
In seat or assigned area	No noises while waiting
Signal/Hand up	Use pleasant voice tone
Pleasant face	
Eyes on teacher	

Source: Fister & Kemp, 1994.

T4: What can I do about the students who disrupt during my instruction?

4.8   Responsibility Roles

Have the target student be a timekeeper during a presentation, a notetaker during a lesson, a recorder of points earned, a facilitator during a cooperative learning group activity, a manager of material distribution, or a counter of teacher praise statements. If appropriate, each time the student performs the role, they can mark on their "role card." The role needs to be clearly defined for the student, with ample practice opportunities provided. Give the student plenty of positive, specific, and descriptive feedback regarding their performance.

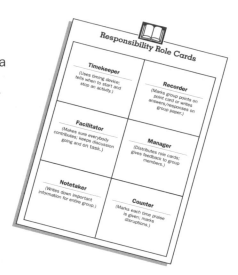

4.9   Countoon

The target students are given a tracker card like the one in the illustration below. Teach them how to identify a disruption and mark it on the card when it occurs. Also teach students a replacement behavior to count and record such as, problems completed, hand raising, or a social skill. The replacement behavior should be an acceptable alternative to the disruptive behavior. Cartoons, hand drawn pictures, or actual photographs representing each behavior are included on each side of the card. Reinforcement for acceptable behavior and daily improvement can be added to this strategy if necessary. (See Mystery Motivators and Wild Card/Spinners under T3.)

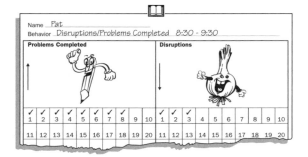

Source: Fister & Kemp, 1994.

T4: What can I do about the students who disrupt during my instruction?

5.1 Highlighting

 Immediately following teacher-directed instruction, have students review important information by using highlighter pens to identify key concepts and facts. Use different color pens or predetermined markings for vocabulary words, dates, formulas, etc. This technique can be done individually or with partners.

EXAMPLES

- Highlight vocabulary words in **yellow** or (Circle.)
- Highlight dates in **pink** or <u>Underline</u>.
- Highlight formulas in **blue** or Box.

5.2 Recycling

 As information is being presented throughout a lesson, stop every two to three minutes and ask questions that the group can answer in unison. It is a good idea to go back to the beginning of the task and ask review questions each time you stop to recycle. This provides cumulative review throughout the lesson and allows students to verbally practice small chunks of information during instruction.

EXAMPLES

- "Get ready to name all the capitals of the eastern states as a group."
- "Let us review the steps needed to solve this word problem together."

5.3 Mnemonics

 A mnemonic is a technique that aids the memory process. There are a variety of mnemonic devices that can be used to remember important concepts and facts.

EXAMPLES

- The names of the Great Lakes can be remembered by using the mnemonic HOMES. Each letter in the word represents one of the lakes.

  Huron
  Ontario
  Michigan
  Erie
  Superior

- The steps in the division process can be taught to students by using this silly sentence: **D**umb **M**onkeys **S**neak **B**ananas.

  Divide
  Multiply
  Subtract
  Bring Down

- Students can develop their own mnemonics by using the **FIRST Letter Mnemonic** strategy. Model and demonstrate the following steps to students.

  Form a word by using the first letter of fact that needs to be remembered.
  Insert a small letter to make a word.
  Rearrange the list if they do not need to be in order.
  Sentence is created to remember the first letters of each word.
  Try a combination of all of the above.

  Source: Nagel, Shumaker, & Deshler, 1986.

5.4   Note Stacks

Have students write questions or facts on one side of an index card and the corresponding information on the other side. This can be done prior to instruction or during the "input" section of the lesson. Keep the cards in piles that can be referenced throughout the unit of instruction.

HOMES	Huron, Ontario Michigan, Erie, Superior (The Great Lakes)

5.5 Memory Log

Develop a format for a memory log to use during discussion or lecture. Create the memory log on chart paper and hang in a noticeable place in the room. Electronic chalkboards can also be used for this purpose. As the teacher is talking, have a student, an assistant, or another teacher record the important information in the memory log. Categories to be included in the log might be: topic, rationale, outcome, important facts and concepts, supporting details, dates to remember, etc. Logs can be used for one lesson only or throughout a unit by adding information each day. Individual versions of memory logs can also be developed and kept in student folders for personal reference.

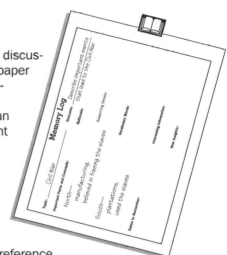

5.6 Study Guides (Standard)

Study guides can be used as an advanced organizer for what is going to be presented in the lesson, as well as review sheets for remembering important concepts taught. The following steps are involved in creating a study guide.

Step 1: Develop an outline of the important facts and concepts to be presented during this portion of the lesson.

Step 2: Arrange the information in statement or question format.

Step 3: Allow students to use the outline to record the important information.

Review the completed study guide with the students at the end of the lesson and prior to teaching the next concept.

Study Guide—Chapter 30
Fishes

1. List two fish that belong to the class Agnatha.
2. Are lampreys parasitic in their larval stage?_____ Adult stage? _____
3. Define spawning.
4. List common characteristics of both lampreys and hagfish.
5. List fishes that have cartilaginous skeletons.
6. The placoderm is an evolutionary link between what two classes of fishes?
7. Which of the ray's fins resemble wings?
8. What are placoid scales?
9. What do sharks eat?
10. Which are the most numerous of modern fishes?
11. What is the function of the swim bladder?

Source: Lovitt, Fister, Kemp, Moore, & Schroeder, 1992.

T5: What can I do about the students who forget information that I presented yesterday or a few hours ago?

5.7 Graphic Organizers (Top Down)

Graphic organizers are visual displays of information that students can complete while the lesson is being presented or following the teachers presentation. They can be used as review or completed while the lesson is presented.

Step 1: Determine important facts and concepts.

Step 2: Arrange them in sequential and logical order.

Step 3: Create a visual display of the information using boxes and pictures.

Step 4: Label reference points

The organizer below demonstrates how information can be visually arranged to further illustrate points made during instruction.

Objective: Define and discuss the early signs and prevention of strokes.

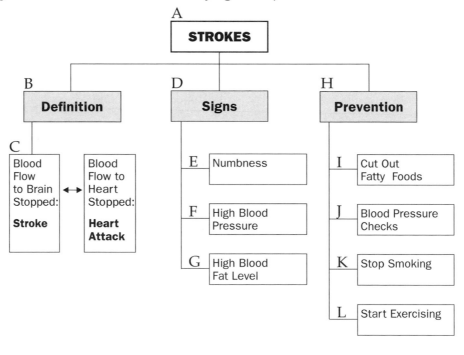

Source: Lovitt et al., 1992.

6.1   Rationale Questions

Include daily review questions and/or test questions related to the "why" aspect of the objective. Rationale questions can be as important as content area questions for skill maintenance. Test questions could include: "List two reasons why this is important."; "Describe when you could use these skills."; or "Describe what you might be able to do with these skills in ten years."

6.2   Think and Say Why

After providing students with a variety of reasons why a skill is important, ask them to write or state reasons (why instruction on a topic is important) during a one-minute timing. This can serve as a useful way to involve students and generate a more comprehensive list of reasons for learning a skill. Reasons can be posted as reminders for the students.

6.3   Share Your Reasons

Ask students to **think** of reasons why the lesson objective is important. This should first be done on their own for ten to 30 seconds. Then, students **pair up** to share their reasons with a partner, and finally, **share** reasons aloud with a group of four or the entire class. Of the pair, one student acts as the reporter in sharing aloud their reasons.

Source: Kagan, 1990.

6.4   What, Where/When, and Why Strategy

Provide students with a What, Where/When, and Why Strategy card such as the one in the illustration. The students will fill in the card with What and Why statements or key words. Instruct students at the beginning of the lesson What they will be able to do with their new knowledge that they cannot do presently. For example: "You will be able to use the steps for getting the teacher's attention."; or "You will be able to say four new words and definitions."; or "You will be able to solve a new variety of word problem."; or "You will be able to identify both similarities and differences in the two characters from our story." Then, have students fill in the What box with what they will be able to do. They might write: use steps, or say words and definitions, or solve problems, or write about same-different qualities.

T6: What can I do about the students who fail to see the relevance of my instruction?

Likewise, tell students at the beginning of the lesson **Where** and/or **When** they can use the **What**. Provide students with situations where they can use the skill. For example, "You can use this strategy in this classroom and other classrooms, in the cafeteria, and at home." Or, "You can use these words when you read the story." Then, instruct students to fill in the **Where/When** box with information on where and when they will be able to use the skill. They might write: in the classroom, at home, on the playground, etc.

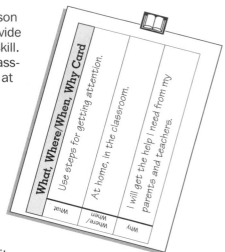

Next, tell students at the beginning of the lesson **Why** the **What** is important. Provide students with a personal benefit (PB) rationale statement, an avoiding a negative consequence (ANC) benefit, or an affect on others (AOO) benefit.

EXAMPLES

- **PB:** "When you use the steps for getting the teacher's attention, you will get the help you need from me and get your work done on time."

- **ANC:** "When you use the steps for getting the teacher's attention, you will not lose points or lose your free time privileges."

- **AOO:** "When you use the steps for getting the teacher's attention, I appreciate a respect that kind of responsible behavior. So will other teachers. That's called a teacher-pleasing behavior!"

Then, instruct students to fill in one of the **Why** boxes with an appropriate rationale statement. What, Where/When, Why cards can be practiced and reviewed before instruction and stored in a folder, notebook, or a ring clip.

6.5   Futures Map

Begin by providing students with a relevant goal for the future that has a connection to the current lesson objectiv Create a Futures Map (see illustration) where you and the students chart the relevance of lessons as "Life Skills." Some of the categories on the map should include: Employment, Leisure/Social Recreation; and Daily Independent Living. The map should also include the lesson objective and how it can be applied both in and out of the classroom. In charting the map, ask students, "What do you see yourself doing in ten years?"; or "What do you want to have accomplished?" Proceed from the future vision back to the present, asking questions like, "What did you need to get there in terms of money, job, education, etc." This activity often helps to establish the relevancy of current lessons when students fail to see the importance.

T6: What can I do about the students who fail to see the relevance of my instruction?

7.1 Positive and Negative Examples

 Several methods of presenting positive and negative examples can be used depending upon the concept being taught and the grade level of the student.

1. A method that is used often with older students is teaching vocabulary through **synonyms**. This procedure includes:

    • Presenting the new word by equating it with a known word.

    • Testing through the use of positive and negative examples.

    • Reviewing the new word with previously introduced words.

Teacher	Students
a. Teacher states the new word and the equivalent, familiar word and then tests.	
1. "Here is a new word: **sturdy**. Sturdy means strong."	
2. "What does sturdy mean?" (Signal.)	"Strong."
b. Teacher presents positive and negative examples until the students make six consecutive correct responses. Examples are not repeated in the same order.	
1. "Tom leaned against a pole. The pole fell over. Was the pole sturdy or not sturdy?" (Signal.)	"Not sturdy."
2. "Tom leaned against another pole. The pole did not move. Was the pole sturdy or not sturdy?" (Signal.)	"Sturdy."
3. "A house did not shake at all in a strong windstorm. Was the house sturdy or not sturdy?" (Signal.)	"Sturdy."
4. "A different house fell down when the wind started blowing. Was the house sturdy or not sturdy?" (Signal.)	"Not sturdy."
(Note: The teacher can also provide practice by asking the students to generate examples. "Tell me about something that is sturdy.")	

T7: What can I do about the students who, following my instruction, do not understand or misgeneralize the concept?

Teacher	Students

c.   Teacher reviews new word and other previously introduced words.

    1.   "Is it mild out today? How do you know?"

    2.   "Is that bench sturdy? How do you know?"

    3.   "Is my desk tidy? How do you know?"

In constructing definitions, teachers must make them understandable to students, rather than make them technically correct. For example, a liquid might be defined as "something poured." Although scientists might disapprove of this definition, it is adequate to teach the meaning of liquid to young children. Definitions are also kept understandable by using words that students understand.

Some sample definitions appear below. Note the effort to keep them as simple as possible.

	Category/Group	Differs from other things in the category/group
Container	An object	you can put things in.
Vehicle	An object	that can take you places.
Seam	A thing	where two pieces of material are sewn together.
Glare	A facial expression	at someone as if you are angry.

Source: Adapted from Carnine, Silbert, & Kameenui, 1990.

2.   **Modeling** is used when it is impossible to find the language to explain the exact meaning of a word. It is used primarily to teach concepts like color, size, and shape covered in preschool and kindergarten. The basic procedures include:

- Providing positive and negative examples of the new concept.

- Testing the students on their mastery of the examples for the new word.

- Presenting different examples of the new word, along with examples of previously taught words.

T7: What can I do about the students who, following my instruction, do not understand or misgeneralize the concept?

	OBJECT	ADJECTIVE (COLOR)	ADVERB	ADJECTIVE (TEXTURE)
Step 1: Teacher models positive and negative examples.	"This is a **mitten**."; or "This is not a mitten." **Examples:** - brown wool mitten - brown wool glove - red nylon glove - red nylon mitten - blue sock - blue mitten	"This is **orange**."; or "This is not orange." **Examples:** - 2" red disk - 2" orange disk - 4" x 4" orange paper - 4" x 4" brown paper	"This is writing **carefully**."; or "This is not writing carefully." **Examples:** - Write on board, first neatly, then sloppily. - Hang up coat, first carefully, then carelessly. - Arrange books, first carelessly, then carefully.	"This is rough." **Examples:** - red flannel shirt - red silk shirt - piece of sandpaper - piece of paper - smooth book cover - rough book cover
Step 2: Teacher tests. Present positive and negative examples until the students make six consecutive correct responses.	"Is this a mitten or not a mitten?"	"Is this orange or not orange?"	"Is this _____ carefully or not carefully?"	"Is this rough or not rough?"
Step 3: Teacher tests by asking for names. Present examples until the students make six consecutive correct responses.	"What is this?" **Examples:** - glove - mitten - sock - mitten - mitten - glove	"What color is this?" - orange - brown - orange - red	"Show me how you _____ carefully."; or "Tell me about how I am writing." (quickly, slowly, carefully, etc.).	"Find the _____ that is rough."; or "Tell me about this shirt." (rough, red, pretty, etc.).

Source: Reprinted with the permission of Macmillian College Publishing Company from *Direct Instruction Reading, 2nd ed.* by Douglas Carnine, Jerry Silbert, and Edward J. Kameenui. © 1990 by Macmillian College Publishing.

7.2   **Strategies and Rules**

When introducing a new concept to students, use consistent vocabulary and provide explicit step-by-step instructions. Students should be taught strategies they can learn relatively easily and can apply to a range of related problems.

EXAMPLES

- **Math Strategies/Rules:**

    1. Reading Thousand Numbers: The number in front of the comma tells how many thousands.

    2. Subtraction With Renaming: When we take away more than we start with, we must rename.

T7: What can I do about the students who, following my instruction, do not understand or misgeneralize the con-cept?

3. Fractions: If the top number is more than the bottom number, the fraction equals more than one whole. If the top number is less than the bottom number, the fraction equals less than one whole.

4. Metric Conversions: When we change to a bigger unit, we divide. When we change to a smaller unit, we multiply.

Source: Silbert, Carnine, & Stein, 1990.

• **Reading Strategies/Rules:**

1. Identifying the Main Idea: If it tells about the whole passage, it is the main idea.

2. Vowel Consonant Silent 'e' (VCe): When there is an 'e' at the end of the word, this letter (vowel) says its name.

3. Writing a Main Idea Sentence: Name the person and tell the main thing the person did in all the sentences.

4. Double Consonants Following a Vowel: If double consonants come after the vowel pronounce the sound (hopping); if a single consonant comes after, pronounce its name (hoping).

Source: Carnine et al., 1990.

7.3   Corrective Feedback

Using a specific strategy for feedback gives the teacher an opportunity to reteach a concept to a student.

EXAMPLE

• A student has been asked the question: "What is the capital of Utah?" and responds, "Provo." Use the following correction procedure to treat the student with dignity and respect while providing a correct answer to the question.

Step 1:   Dignify the Response—Do this by moving close to the student, using the student's name, and maintaining a pleasant voice tone and facial expression. Use phrases such as, "You are thinking of another large city in Utah that is farther south than the capital."; or "I wonder if you are thinking of . . . ." If the answer does not make sense to you, use phrases such as, "Help me understand how you came up with that answer."; or "I am not sure what you are thinking, can you tell me?"

Step 2:   Correct the Answer—Do this by prompting the student for the answer. An example might be: "This city starts with an 'S' and has three words."; or give the student the answer, "The capital of Utah is Salt Lake City."

Step 3:   Validate the Student's Response—Do this by having the student give the correct answer before you move on to another question or student. Let the student know that you will be back to them later to see if they remember the correct answer.

7.4 Concept Angles

When using the right angle diagram, instruct students to insert the concept being taught on the **right arrow** and related information about the concept on the **down arrow**. Have the students share this information with a partner or report to the entire class to check for understanding of the concept.

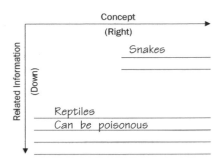

Source: Bellanca & Fogarty, 1991.

7.5 Plus, Minus, Interesting (PMI)

When using the chart below, have students fill out each category immediately following the teachers presentation. In the **P** (Plus) column tell the students to write down all the ideas/concepts they absolutely understand. The **M** (Minus) column can represent the information that students are still unclear on. The **I** (Interesting) column indicates concepts they understand, but find interesting and want to explore in more depth. The **PMI** categories can be changed to meet the teachers need and subject area. After the charts have been completed, post them around the room or share them aloud with the class.

Topic: Algebra

P+	Inequalities: $2x < 6 \rightarrow x < 3$
M-	Factoring: $x^2 + 2x + 1 = (x + 1)^2$
I?	Absolute values are always positive: $|-x| = x$

Source: Bellanca & Fogarty, 1991.

7.6 I Question That!

Provide students with the following chart to fill out as the information is being presented. Review what students have written down with the entire class. This is especially useful when difficult vocabulary keeps students from understanding the concepts.

Topic: _Hamlet by William Shakespeare: Soliloquy "To be, or not to be ...."_

What Do I Think Is Being Said?	What Words Keep Me From Understanding?
Hamlet is debating whether or not to commit suicide.	"consummation" line 63 "fardels" line 76 "the native hue of resolution" line 84

T7: What can I do about the students who, following my instruction, do not understand or misgeneralize the concept?

7.7   **Know/Want to Know/Learned (KWL)**

Give students the following chart to fill out before and after the information is presented. Discuss the responses with partners, cooperative groups or the entire class.

Topic: _____Sewing_____

What We Know.	What We Want to Find Out.	What We Learned.
How to thread a sewing machine	How to use a serger	How to create french seams

Source: Bellanca & Fogarty, 1991.

7.8   **Learning Logs**

Have students write in a notebook for a specified amount of time (five minutes) during the lesson or immediately following. Use the following questions or make up your own. You can also use illustrations or icons as questions (e.g., a lightbulb, smiling face, question marks).

1. What did I learn?

2. What puzzled me?

3. What did I not enjoy?

4. How did I learn?

5. What will I remember most?

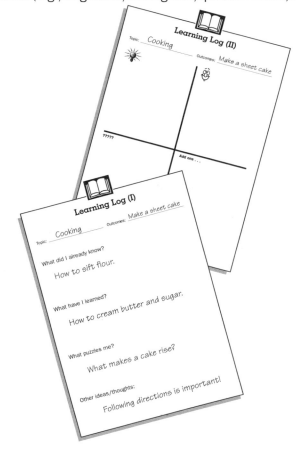

T7: What can I do about the students who, following my instruction, do not understand or misgeneralize the concept?

7.9 Study Guides (Margins)

Study Guides help students stay focused during a lesson and provide a logical structure to the concepts being presented. The margins provide a space for students to write more notes. They can also indicate page numbers in a book where information can be found. The following steps can be used to develop study guides.

Step 1: Develop an outline of the important facts and concepts to be presented during this portion of the lesson.

Step 2: Arrange the information in statement or question format.

Step 3: Allow students to use the outline to record the important information.

Study Guide—Chapter 8
Sponges

1. What does the phylum name porifera literally mean?

2. Define sessile.

3. Sponge Spicules may be made of what two substances?

4. Name the largest sponge. How big is it?

5. How many species of sponge exist?

6. Define choanocytes.

7. Name the three canal systems found in sponges.

8. What does it mean to be a filter feeder?

Source: Lovitt et al., 1992.

7.10 Graphic Organizers (Sequence)

Graphic organizers display information spatially and connect concepts for students in a meaningful way. An organizer can be used to link new information to past learnings and help students organize and focus on the most important concepts of the lesson. The following steps can be used to develop a graphic organizer:

Step 1: Determine important facts and concepts.

Step 2: Arrange them in sequential and logical order.

Step 3: Create a visual display of the information using boxes and pictures.

Step 4: Label reference points.

The Battle of New Orleans

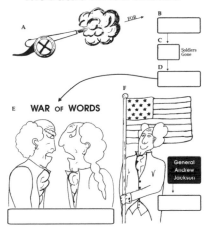

Graphic organizers can be used to present concepts in a Top Down-Bottom Up format (main ideas and supporting details), a Compare and Contrast format (comparison of several critical attributes), a Sequence format (progression of events over time), or a Diagram format (charts, graphs, maps, or picture representations).

Source: Lovitt et al., 1992.

7-11   Attribute Maps

Use an Attribute Map during instruction to provide examples and nonexamples of the concept being taught. First, supply students with a definition of the concept to be discussed. Then, describe the critical attributes or characteristics that apply to the concept. For instance in the illustration below, the first column is a list of attributes or characteristics that are **always** present among insects. The second column lists attributes that are **sometimes** present and the last column lists attributes that are **never** present among insects. The teacher then gives three to six examples and nonexamples of insects using information the students are already familiar with or have been taught. Attribute Maps can be used as review sheets or as a measure of a student's understanding of a concept.

Insects		
Definition: **A group of small animals belonging to the arthropods.**		
ALWAYS	SOMETIMES	NEVER
three body parts three pairs of legs	two pairs of wings	backbone

EXAMPLES	NONEXAMPLES
Flies Mosquitoes Grasshoppers Beetles Butterflies	Spider Centipede Snail Mites Ticks

T7: What can I do about the students who, following my instruction, do not understand or misgeneralize the concept?

8.1   Group/Individual Questioning

 Instruct students that you will call for a **group** response for a task before calling on an **individual** student to respond. Consistency with this approach creates a less threatening environment and allows students to hear a correct response before being called upon.

8.2   Responses Without Talking

 Allow students who are unable or reluctant to give verbal responses to use an alternative response.

EXAMPLES

- Write their response on paper or a small chalkboard.

- Give a hand signal response like signing, thumbs up, or pointing.

- Hold up a card with a word or number response like a math answer, true-false, agree-disagree, a letter or sound, etc.

8.3   I am Ready

 Allow students to have additional time to think of responses.

For example, tell them to give you a signal like putting an index finger on their forehead or standing up a card on their desk to alert you that they are ready with answers.

T8: What can I do about the students who do not volunteer information during my instruction?

8.4　Please Come Back

Teach students that if called upon to answer and they do not have a response, they say, **"Please come back,"** or put up a sign that reads the same. The student should understand that saying, "I do not know," is not an option. "Please come back," allows the student additional time to think, research an answer, or confer with a partner or group for assistance. Additional prompts can also be provided for the student in order to guarantee a successful response. Remember to come back to the student and provide praise for a correct response.

8.5　Name's Up Volunteer Board

A Name's Up Volunteer Board is a place where the teacher can quickly write/post students' names when they volunteer information or responses. The board can be a portion of the chalkboard, a flip chart, or a white board (see illustration below). When the teacher notices volunteering behaviors (e.g., hand raising, contributing relevant information with other students, responding in unison with the entire class or group, correct responses, etc.) the student's name is written on the Volunteer Board and the teacher verbally recognizes the behavior with an enthusiastic description of the behavior. ("Wow, look at Charles. He is participating and contributing answers!") When students demonstrate subsequent volunteering information behaviors, the teacher can simply put check marks (✓) next to their name as the praise is delivered. At the end of the instructional period, the names can be erased and the activity repeated.

Volunteer Board	
Charles	
Susan	
Ray	✓ ✓
Janet	✓

8.6　Heads Together

Students are arranged in groups of four. Each group member is assigned a number (one-four) or a color. The teacher presents a question to the entire class and tells each group of four to put their heads together and come up with an answer in which all members agree. The teacher then asks all of the ones (or twos, threes, fours) who have an answer to raise their hands or stand up. The teacher then calls on one in the group to respond. The teacher can then ask the ones in the other groups if they agree, disagree, or to expand on the answer. The teacher can then repeat this process with all numbers or colors.

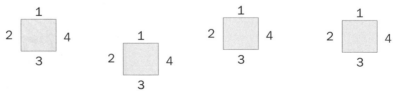

Source: Kagan, 1990.

T8: What can I do about the students who do not volunteer information during my instruction?

8.7 Folded Corners

Students are placed in groups of four. Each group puts their team name in the middle of one piece of paper. Each team member then writes their name on one corner of the paper and folds it over. The papers are passed to the teacher to be used when calling on nonvolunteers. The teacher asks a question to the entire class, allows the teams a few seconds to share their ideas, draws one of the papers, lifts one corner, and calls on that student to respond.

Source: Kagan, 1990.

8.8 Draw-a-Name

Put each student's name on a ticket, index card, or Popsicle stick. Students who need more opportunities to respond or those who infrequently volunteer information can have their name written on at least four tickets or cards. The tickets, cards, or sticks are then put in a container. When the teacher wants to ask questions or call on nonvolunteers, they use the following steps:

Step 1: **Ask** the question.

Step 2: **Pause** to give three to five seconds of thinking time.

Step 3: **Draw** a name from the container.

Step 4: **Call** on the student whose name was drawn.

Step 5: **Listen** to the student's response.

Step 6: **Provide** descriptive praise to the student.

T8: What can I do about the students who do not volunteer information during my instruction?

9.1 Think About That

When asking questions to the class, use the following strategy along with providing additional thinking time.

Step 1: **Ask** the question to the entire class. "What operation would you use to solve this math problem? Think about that."

Step 2: **Pause** and allow additional think time. "Touch your forehead when you have an answer."; or "Raise your pencil when you are ready."

Step 3: **Call** on the entire class as a group or solicit individual responses.

9.2 All Talk Together

First have students respond in unison as a group in order to "firm-up" answers. The group responses can be verbal, nonverbal or written. Then call on the target student to give the answer. See Everybody Say in T4.1.

9.3 Think, Pair, Share

After asking a question, have students:

- **Think** on their own about the answer.
- **Pair** up with another student.
- **Share** their responses with each other.

Giving students an opportunity to share with each other will help to ensure that the target students will have responses when called upon.

Source: Kagan, 1990.

T9: What can I do about the students who make hesitant responses or frequent errors during my instruction?

9.4   Formulate, Share, Listen, Create

After a question has been posed, have the students:

- **Formulate** an answer individually.

- **Share** the answer with a partner.

- **Listen** to their partner's answer.

- **Create** a new answer through discussion.

The teacher then calls on an individual for the response.

Source: Johnson, Johnson, & Bartlett, 1990.

9.5   Prompts

When the student hesitates, provide clues that will assist in the retrieval of the answer. Prompts can be memory strategies, a rule, or part of the answer.

EXAMPLES

- "What is the capital of Vermont?" (Student hesitates.) "The capital begins with the second syllable in the word Vermont.

- "Does this problem require regrouping?" (Student is slow to respond.) "Remember the rule: When we take away more than we start with, we must regroup."

9.6   Prequestioning

Provide students with a list of questions that will be asked during the presentation. Allow students to review them prior to the class discussion and find the answers if necessary.

9.7   Please Come Back

When students do not have the answer when called upon, teach them the "Please Come Back" technique. This gives students time to formulate their answers or think on their options. See T8.4 for more ideas.

9.8   Rapid-Fire Questions

Have each student respond aloud to review information. The teacher moves quickly around the room asking questions. If a student makes an error or hesitates, he or she is told the correct answer and the teacher moves to the next student and response/question. If all questions have been answered, the teacher starts over and continues around the room until students have responded many times to the questions.

EXAMPLES

- "Let us review the steps in the notetaking process. Starting with John, state the first letter 'L' and the first step, Listen. Sally will say the next letter 'l' and the corresponding step, Identify. We will continue until all steps have been named and then the next person will start over again. Keep it going until I say 'stop.'"

- "Name one thing you remember about yesterday's presentation."

The Rapid-Fire method can also be used with math facts, vocabulary, etc. This can be an effective active review techique.

9.9   Think and Say Ideas

Give students a specific topic or concept that has recently been presented (e.g., Natural Resources, Rhyming Words, States and Capitals). Have them think quietly about the topic for a few minutes, then either share aloud to a partner or write down all of their ideas related to the topic during a two- to three-minute timing. Have students share the ideas generated with the class. Do this activity throughout the lesson to build the students' fluency on the topic.

9.10   Up the Numbers

Have students pick a goal from one to ten for the number of questions they will answer during the teacher's presentation. After the lesson, have students determine whether they met their goal or not. Encourage them to up their number by one for the next lesson. The presentation must include an ample number of opportunities for all students to respond in order for them to achieve their goal. This can be done by having students respond as a class, a row, a table, as well as individually.

9.11   Corrective Feedback

Using a specific strategy for feedback, assists the students in filing the information in their mind to reduce confusion of concepts.

EXAMPLE

- The student has been asked the following question: "Who is the main character in the story *The Tangled Web*?" The student responds, "Josefa." (The answer is Annie.) Use the following correction procedure to treat the student with dignity and respect and provide a correct answer to the question.

    Step 1:   Dignify the Response—The teacher does this by moving close to the student, using the student's name, and maintaining a pleasant voice tone and facial expression. Use phrases such as: "You are thinking of another character that is in the story . . . ."; or "I wonder if you are thinking of . . . . " If the answer does not make sense, the teacher uses phrases such as: "Help me understand how you came up with that answer"; or "I am not sure what you are thinking, can you tell me?"

    Step 2:   Correct the Answer—The teacher does this by prompting the student for the answer. An example might be, "This character is also a girl and her name starts with A." Or he or she may give the student the answer, "The main character is Annie."

    Step 3:   Validate the Student's Response—The teacher does this by having the student give the correct answer before moving on to another question or student. The teacher lets the student know that he or she will be back later to see if the student remembers the correct answer.

9.12 The Question Challenge

Challenge students to correctly answer fact questions during the presentation. The teacher tells them that he or she will be asking both group and individual questions and will keep score on the board. If the students answer the question correctly, they receive a point. If the group hesitates or makes an error, the response is corrected and the point is awarded to the teacher. Develop the questions beforehand and prepare the students for the type of questions that will be asked. A suggested guideline for number of questions asked is four to six per minute. Playing this game often will build fluency and reduce errors in student responses.

Approximate Number of Questions: 30	
Students	Ms. Jones
~~IIII~~ ~~IIII~~ I	~~IIII~~ III

T9: What can I do about the students who make hesitant responses or frequent errors during my instruction?

10.1   Buddy Carbon Notes

Provide capable notetakers with carbon paper to record a second copy of the class notes for buddies who are not able to write down information. The carbon copy of notes can be given to the buddy after the presentation. The student who has difficulty writing down information can be involved during the presentation by using a graphic organizer or study guide to write down limited information, or simply highlight.

10.2   Four-Fold

Provide students with a four-fold like the one in the illustration. Students can simply fold a piece of paper into four parts or preformatted sheets can be distributed.

Step 1:   In the upper left box, students record their name, date, topic, and lesson objective.

Step 2:   In the upper right box, students record a personal relevance statement after the teacher's presentation. This is a statement that answers the question, "What personal meaning does this information have for you in your life?"

Step 3:   In the lower left box, the students number and record the main ideas from the teacher's presentation.

Step 4:   In the lower right box, the students number and record supporting details (i.e., definitions, examples, nonexamples, clarifications) related to the main ideas.

It is important that the teacher use an overhead transparency of a blank four-fold and model this procedure as information is presented to the students.

10.3 Index Cards

During the teacher's presentation, students are instructed by the teacher to write down key vocabulary words or phrases on one side of an index card and the corresponding definition on the back side. Students keep the cards in a file box or on a ring for later use during guided and independent practice activities.

10.4 Slotted Outline

An outline or study guide (see the illustration below) of the teacher's lecture can be prepared leaving blank spaces where key vocabulary or concepts can be written in by the student as the teacher is presenting the information. The teacher can model the procedure using an overhead transparency of the outline by filling in the spaces as each item is presented.

Study Guide—Chapter 3
Chemistry

1. The first element on the periodic table is _____ and its abbreviation is _____ .

2. There are _____ elements on the periodic table.

3. The atomic number of carbon is _____ .

4. _____ indicates how many protons the element has.

5. Au is the abbreviation for _____ .

10.5 LITES

Model the LITES strategy for students when giving students new information and concepts. Use an overhead transparency of the notetaking outline similar to the one in the illustration. Students can be given a bookmark with the LITES strategy spelled out to serve as a prompt to take notes while reading.

Listen to the teacher and look at what he or she is saying aloud and writing.

Identify key vocabulary, important concepts, and examples/nonexamples that the teacher is using or saying aloud.

Take down (write down) the key vocabulary, concepts, and examples.

Evaluate what has been taken down. Ask yourself questions like: Could I explain this to someone? Could I give more examples? If not, put a question mark in the left margin and use your strategy for asking a question or asking for a clarification.

Save your notes by dating them, coding chapters or topics, and putting them in a folder or notebook.

Remember that it will be necessary to actively teach and model the LITES strategy while using the notetaking outlines (see illustration). It will require several weeks of prompted practice before students will be able to use this strategy independently.

T10: *What can I do about the students who have difficulty taking notes during my instruction?*

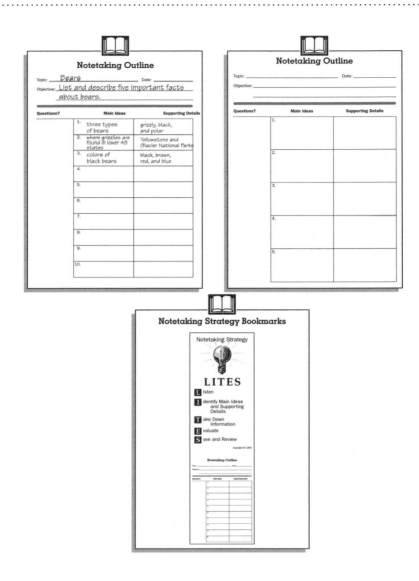

10.6 Note Checks

Develop a daily point system for taking notes or using a notetaking outline (described in LITES T10.6). These points should be tied to students' participation grades. Points can also be awarded for dating the notes, coding the notes to chapters or topics, and maintaining them in an orderly fashion in folders or notebooks. Note checks can occur on a regular basis or be used as unannounced random checks.

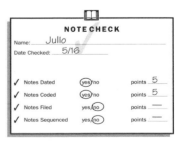

T10: What can I do about the students who have difficulty taking notes during my instruction?

10.7 Cooperative Notes

Arrange students into groups of four for the teacher's presentation. Each student is assigned a number (one through four) and the group is provided with one set of paper for taking notes (see illustration). All number ones begin with the note paper, writing down their name and start time as shown in the illustration. The teacher sets a timer for five minutes and all number ones begin taking notes. At the end of five minutes, the note paper rotates to the number two person and the procedure is repeated throughout teacher-directed instruction. At the end of each time block the teacher can provide feedback to the students on the notes by showing a transparency modeling an example set of notes for the previous five minute time block. The notetaker can check his or her notes with the model and add or delete information. At the end of the notetaking session, groups can switch notes for other activities such as editing, evaluating, or rewriting.

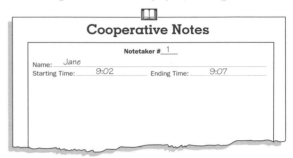

10.8 Graphic Organizers (Partial)

Provide students with a blank, partially completed, or completely filled out graphic organizer of the teacher's presentation (see illustration below). As the teacher is presenting information, students can fill in or add important information on their copy of the organizer.

For example, a completely filled out version of the graphic organizer can be given to students who have limited writing skills. They can be given a highlighter pen and be required to mark the key concepts as information is presented and/or add additional words next to the boxes. Other students can use a partially completed or blank organizer when they are required to write down additional information. (See T5.7 for completed organizer on strokes.)

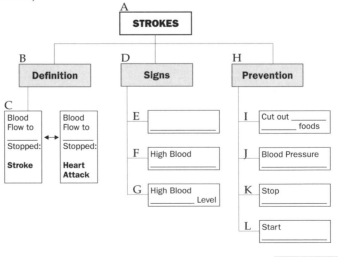

Source: Lovitt et al., 1992.

T10: What can I do about the students who have difficulty taking notes during my instruction?

11.1 Defend Your Position

Split the class in two and have one group listen for what they believe to be the positive statements or concepts related to the topic; the other group listens for the negative concepts or implications. Then, each group writes down their choices and supporting information. Next, allow each group to present their position. This information can be written down by the teacher and displayed in the room for later reference by students.

Topic: The Power of Language	
Positive	**Negative**
a way for human beings to communicate	can be misunderstood

11.2 Five-Minute Reviews

Set a timer to ring every five minutes. When the timer rings, stop the presentation to review the critical information presented to that point. Have students compare what they have recorded with a partner and give time to add any information that was not included in their notes. Ask questions (individual and group) related to the critical information to discover if students have interpreted it correctly or show an overhead transparency that has been completed with the critical information.

11.3   Advance Organizers

Provide students with organizers that will alert them in advance to the important information that will be presented in class. Explain to the students how the completed outline will be used during instruction.

Topic _____the heart_____

Vocabulary Words:

1. ventricle
2. atrium
3. pulmonary

Key Concepts:

- Ventricles pump blood into atrium.

- Ventricles and atrium make up four chambers of human heart.

- Pulmonary vein carries blood from the heart to the lungs.

Other Important Facts:

11.4   Think and Write Questions

Prior to the presentation, have students **think** of and **write** down questions related to what they want to know about this topic or what they think may be presented. The questions are related to the who, what, when, where, and why of the upcoming material. The teacher adds any questions that have not been suggested, but are critical to students' understanding. As a final step, the teacher assists the students in rearranging the questions or topics into the sequence in which it will be presented.

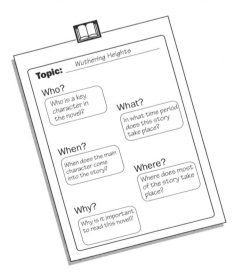

11.5 Presentation Cues

Teach students different types of cues that can be used by the teacher during a presentation. Discuss both spoken and unspoken cues. After teaching students the cues, play games with lectures to see who can identify how many cues were used and/or what the cues were. The following chart provides some presentation cues for students.

	Verbal	**Nonverbal**
Emphasis	"This is important!" "You will need to remember _____." "This will be on the test." Repeating information Voice inflections Volume of voice Pacing of information	Signals: • Pointing • Hand movement Facial expressions Body language Other gestures
Organization	"The first step is _____." "Number three _____." "Next _____." "In summary _____."	Writing on board Gestures Pauses Finger counting

T11: What can I do about the students who have a difficult time determining the critical information from my instruction?

12.1 Ask, Pause, Call

Ask the question to the entire group, **pause** at least three to five seconds for think time, and then **call** on a student or group for a response.

EXAMPLE

- **Ask**, "Class, get ready to recite the rule for regrouping."

- **Pause** to give students think time, "Raise your hand or touch your forehead when you are ready to give the rule."

- **Call** on an individual student, small group, or the entire class for the response.

12.2 Restate

Ask the student or entire class to restate the question that has been presented. Or, ask the student or class to restate the answer to the question after another student has responded correctly.

EXAMPLES

- "Class, get ready to repeat my question. What is another way of saying 'minus'?"

- "Susan, repeat Mark's answer in your own words."

You can also tell students ahead of time that you are going to play restate for points. When a student or the class can restate correctly, a class point is earned. If the student or class is incorrect, the teacher earns a point.

12.3 Pass for Now

This is the same strategy as discussed in "Please Come Back." See T8.4 for more information on how to apply its principles to unresponsive students.

T12: What can I do about the students who do not respond to my questions?

12.4 Consult

Teach students to quickly and quietly choose and consult with another person when they need assistance with an answer. When a student is called upon and they are unable to respond, they can say, "consult" and then quickly choose a helping partner.

This technique empowers students and can be used in place of the teacher saying, "Who can help Susan?"

12.5 All Together

Use choral, unison, group, or entire class responses before calling on individual students. Tell students you will be using the all together strategy and review the procedure with them:

- Use talking voices, not shouting voices.

- Respond when the teacher gives you a signal to respond, not before or after the signal.

The teacher can use signals such as a verbal cue and a hand drop or finger touch to keep students in unison. For example, "Get ready to recite the words, what word?" (finger touch) "Next word," (finger touch) etc. If students do not respond in unison, use a pleasant voice tone, then the item should be repeated until the desired unison response is obtained. The teacher can add variety and fun to the verbal responses by asking students to recite (the word or task) in their softest voices, their deepest voices, or their highest voices.

12.6 No Surprises

Prearrange a subtle, no surprise signal with target students that can be used to cue them in advance of being called upon. For example, you might arrange with a student that when you are standing next to his or her desk, you will be calling on him or her next.

12.7 Answer, Pair, Spotlight

After presenting the question, instruct students to think of an **answer** on their own for 30 to 60 seconds, then **pair** with a partner and quietly share responses with each other. Next, use a **spotlighting** technique by calling on pairs to share their responses. One partner (the reporter) can share both responses. When other pairs are spotlighted they should only report new ideas or information.

12.8 Clarification

Teach the students a strategy to ask for a clarification when they do not understand the question or when they need to have the question restated. For example:

Step 1: Use the strategy for getting the teacher's attention (Look, signal, wait to be acknowledged).

Step 2: Use a pleasant voice tone.

Step 3: Say, "I do not understand the question."; or "Could you please restate the question?"

Step 4: Say, "Thank you."

Each of the steps can be modified to fewer words, or pictures can be used to represent the steps. Rhymes or short phrases can also be used such as, **Listen, wait, then ask for a restate.**

A T-chart can be used to teach students what specific behaviors are necessary for each step.

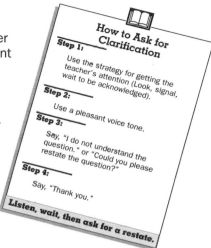

How to Ask for Clarification

Step 1: Use the strategy for getting the teacher's attention (Look, signal, wait to be acknowledged).

Step 2: Use a pleasant voice tone.

Step 3: Say, "I do not understand the question." or "Could you please restate the question?"

Step 4: Say, "Thank you."

Listen, wait, then ask for a restate.

LOOKS LIKE	SOUNDS LIKE
Signal for teacher	No noises while signaling
Pleasant facial expression	Pleasant voice tone
In seat	"I do not understand."
	"Could you please restate?"
	"Thank you."

12.9 Draw-a-Name

This strategy is explained in full in answer T8.8. Please reference for information that can be applied to this question as well.

12.10 Counting Responses

Provide the student with an index card to self-monitor the number of questions answered during a portion of class time. The student can simply mark a box each time a response is given when called upon by the teacher. The boxes can be checked whether the responses are volunteer or nonvolunteer.

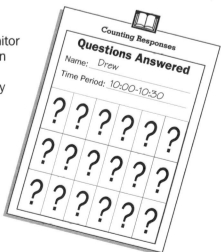

Counting Responses

Questions Answered

Name: *Drew*

Time Period: *10:00–10:30*

? ? ? ? ?
? ? ? ? ?
? ? ? ? ?

T12: What can I do about the students who do not respond to my questions?

Guided Practice Activities

1.1   Effective Praise

Pay attention to the kinds of behavior (or close approximations of the behavior) that is expected of the students. Descriptive praise can be powerful in building responsible student behavior. Use the following procedure to praise students for beginning or completing practice activities:

Step 1: **The teacher should move close to the student and position himself or herself at eye level.** Make eye contact, smile, and touch the student if appropriate. Use the student's name and maintain a pleasant voice tone.

Step 2: **Make a praise statement.** "Susan, nice Job! You must be proud of your responsible behavior."

Step 3: **Describe the student's appropriate behavior.** "Susan, you got started on your assignment right after I gave the instructions, and you are working on the first problem!"

Step 4: **Provide a rationale statement** (optional). "That is important, Susan. When you get your work done, you will know how to do the problems and then you will have time to choose some other activities."

Step 5: **Provide a consequence** (optional). "Susan, you have earned another bonus point on your card for demonstrating responsible behavior."

1.2   Think Out Loud

Check to make sure that the students understand what they need to do in order to complete the assignment or task. The teacher should move in closely and quietly ask each student to restate the instructions and/or explain what needs to be done first, second, and so on.

G1: What can I do about the students who do not begin or complete practice/seatwork activities?

The teacher asks the student to complete one or two items while he or she watches and listens. Instruct the student to think out loud: "Susie, please tell me what the instructions tell you to do."; or "Susie, tell me how you will complete this assignment. What will you do first? What will you do next? How will you know if you have completed all of the steps?" Additionally, the teacher can say, "Now tell me what you are thinking as you work or solve this problem."

The same procedure can be used by having the students turn to a partner and explain the assignment, the instructions, and/or the steps for completing the task.

1.3 Rationale Statements

Sometimes students do not see the importance of starting or finishing an activity. If this is the case, provide them with a meaningful rationale for practicing the skill. Then, make sure that the students can communicate the relevance in their own words to the teacher or to another student.

For instance: "It is important to practice saying these words the fast way so that you will be able to read quickly and understand the story."; or "It is important to practice the steps for getting the teacher's attention so that you will get the help you need."

Additional ideas for helping students understand the relevance of instruction can be found in T6.

1.4 Alternating Buddies

Allow students to pair up for completing practice assignments. Students alternate between writing the answers on and talking through the answer aloud. Partners can initial each item in which they write the answer out.

1.5 Strategic Skills

Rather than asking the students to complete the entire practice assignment, focus on just the strategic skills that are necessary for completing the task.

EXAMPLES

- For a math assignment, ask the students to mark the problems that require regrouping, rather than solve all the problems.

- For a reading assignment, ask the students to indicate page numbers and paragraphs where certain information can be found relating to comprehension, rather than answering all questions.

- For a language assignment, ask the students to list the steps for writing a good paragraph, rather than creating an entire paragraph.

- For a punctuation activity, ask the students to mark the sentences that require capital letters.

1.6   Beat the Clock

Establish reasonable time limits for beginning and/or completing a small number of items on the practice assignment.

EXAMPLES

- Place a timer on the target student's desk. Have the student set the timer for the amount of time estimated to complete the tasks.

- Using a timer, challenge the student. For instance, "Finish these problems in five minutes to beat the clock!"

1.7   Assignment Questions

After distributing practice assignments and explaining the steps for completion, instruct students to think of questions about the assignment and write them down during a two-minute timing. Then, students pair up and share their questions and answers. The teacher then calls for questions that dyads cannot answer on their own. Questions can be answered by the teacher or other dyads.

1.8   Star Stickers

Continually move around the classroom as students are completing a practice activity. As a student starts or completes an item, describe their behavior and then place a star sticker on their practice sheet.

EXAMPLES

- As a student completes a math problem, say something like, "Nice work, you just finished a problem!" Then place a star sticker on that problem.

- As a student writes one sentence during a writing activity, say something like, "Wow, you wrote one sentence and remembered to include the period!" Then place a star sticker at the end of the sentence. (Colored marking pens or a premade ink stamp can also be used in place of stars stickers for the same purpose.)

1.9   Cut-Up

Cut the practice assignment into small strips or pieces. After one piece has been completed, praise the students and then give them the next piece of the assignment.

EXAMPLES

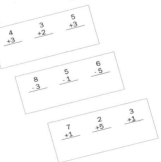

- A page of math problems can be cut up into strips or rows.

- A reading assignment can be cut up into paragraphs.

- A list of comprehension questions can be cut up into individual questions.

- A study guide can be cut up into groups of two or three questions.

G1: What can I do about the students who do not begin or complete practice/seatwork activities?

1.10 Colored Pencils

Give the target student five different colored pencils. Each practice item is completed with a different colored pencil. After five items have been completed, provide the student with a reward. The different colors may make it clearer for the student to see what has been accomplished and provide a goal for reinforcement.

1.11 Split the Assignment

Put students into groups of four or five when working on practice assignments. Each group is given one practice assignment. Each student in the group is responsible for completing a small portion of the task (e.g., questions one to three). The completed tasks are then combined onto one sheet.

Students who are responsible for the same numbered item(s) across all the classroom groups can meet in "expert" groups to complete the task. After they have finished, they return to their "home" group and share the information and record it on the practice assignment.

1.12 Change the Channel

Change the Channel involves changing the **input** and/or the **output** channel that is required in the practice assignment.

EXAMPLES

- A math assignment that requires the student to **look** at math facts on a page and then **write** answers could be changed to:

  1. **Look** at facts and **say** answers aloud.

  2. **Look** at facts and **calculate** answers with a calculator.

  3. **Hear** the facts dictated and **write** answers.

  4. **Hear** the facts dictated and **circle** answers on a piece of paper.

- A reading assignment that requires the student to **look** at words on a page and then **write** definitions for them could be changed to:

  1. **Hear** the word and **say** the definition aloud.

  2. **Hear** the word and **mark** the definition on a sheet of paper.

  3. **See** the word and **say** the definition aloud.

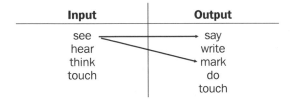

G1: What can I do about the students who do not begin or complete practice/seatwork activities?

1.13 Slice Back

With some students it may be necessary to modify the level of difficulty in the assignment.

EXAMPLE

If the assignment requires students to write paragraphs on a selected topic, the assignment may be more appropriate if students completed a related or parallel activity within the context of the skill area. For instance:

- Circle paragraphs when reading a story.

- Mark the words that describe a certain character.

- Mark the words that tell about the setting.

- Circle the different names of characters.

- Mark other key words.

- Highlight the sentence that describes the content of the whole paragraph.

1.14 Behavior Bingo

Provide the target students with Behavior Bingo Cards (see illustration) and an envelope containing numbered squares that correspond with the numbers on the students' cards. Each time they complete one item on the practice assignment, the teacher draws a number from the envelope and the student places it on the bingo card. When a bingo is achieved, the students earn another reward like one minute of free time or a special privilege.

Source: Jenson et al., 1992.

1.15 Design Your Own

Allow students the option of designing their own practice assignment. Students can complete the Design Your Own form on an individual basis, with a partner, or within the context of a small group. Students are required to provide answers for questions such as: skills they will be practicing, materials they will need, how will they determine if the goal has been met, where and how long they will practice, what student/students are accountable for completing the assignment, and their start and finish estimates. Teacher approval must be obtained after students have designed their own assignment.

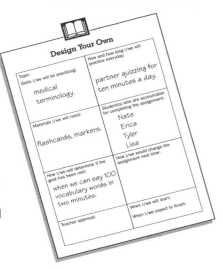

1.16   Assignment Aims

Use a daily assignment aim card like the one in the illustration. The teacher sets a daily aim for each student or the student is asked to set their own. A daily aim consists of completing at least one more item than the student completed the day before on a similar practice assignment. If daily aims are achieved, a pre-determined reward is provided for the students along with a lot of enthusiastic and descriptive praise.

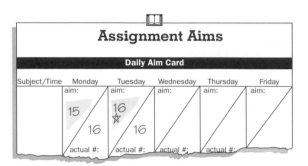

Daily aim cards can be more effective when used in conjunction with Transformer Pens or other invisible inks. Prior to giving the card to the student, the teacher uses the pen to randomly make stars (or other symbols) in several of the boxes. If the daily aim is achieved, the student is allowed to use a Transformer Pen to color in the box. If a star appears, then the student receives another special award.

1.17   Completion Dots

Provide the student with a dot to dot illustration. Each time the student completes a task on a practice activity, a line is connected between dots beginning with number one. This procedure can be combined with the use of Transformer Pens as described in G1.16. Invisible ink stars can be premarked under random dots. The student can use a Transformer Pen to color over dots which have been joined by a connecting line. If a star appears, the student can be given an award.

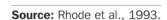

Source: Rhode et al., 1993.

1.18 Ask for Help

Teach students a strategy for how to ask for help when it is apparent that they are unclear on the assignment. Model examples and nonexamples of each of the steps in the strategy. Provide a lot of opportunities for the students to practice the strategy in controlled settings.

Step 1: Use the steps for getting the teacher's attention (Look, signal, wait to be acknowledged).

Step 2: Use a pleasant voice tone.

Step 3: Use the "please" word when requesting help. ("Could you please help me?")

Step 4: Make a specific statement or question about the kind of help you need, where you need help, or what you do not understand ("I need help with this problem.")

Step 5: Smile and say, "Thank you" after help has been given.

Step 6: Ask another specific question if you need more help.

A pleasant request is best, then a thank you does the rest.

1.19 Start/Stop Time

Have the target students use a Start/Stop time card to record when the first assignment or task begins. The ending time is recorded when the assignment or task is finished. The elapsed time is then figured and recorded in the third column. The procedure can be repeated for all items within an assignment. When completed, each student indicates a plus for improvement in time, a minus if the time spent was longer, or a circle if the time was the same. Points can be awarded for improvement times or the number of pluses on the card.

G1: What can I do about the students who do not begin or complete practice/seatwork activities?

Item #	Start Time	Stop Time	Elapsed Time	+	−	◯
1. Sentences	9:00	9:10	10 min.		✓	
2. Paragraphs	9:10	9:15	5 min.	✓		
3.						
4.						
5.						
6.						
7.						
8.						
9.						
10.						

1.20 Monitoring Seatwork

Provide the student with a self-monitoring chart like the one in the illustration. Teach students to slash a number after each problem, item, or task is completed. Provide many opportunities for success by numbering the chart 1-50 for each day. See Counting Responses (T12.10) for additional ideas.

This procedure can be also combined with Assignment Aims and Magic Pens found under G2.

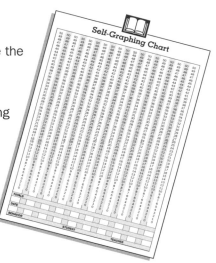

Source: Fister & Kemp, 1994.

G1: What can I do about the students who do not begin or complete practice/seatwork activities?

2.1　Color Coding

This technique works well for oral reading practice with students who tend to look at only part of a word and then make random guesses at its entirety. Determine which part(s) of the word the student is not paying attention to; determine whether it is the beginning, middle, or end. Then **color code** the word by writing that part of the word in a different color or underlining. A highlighter pen can also be used for this purpose. For instance, the beginning of the word can be underlined in green, the middle of the word in yellow, and the end of the word in red to indicate **start**, **caution**, and **stop** points. This technique can also be applied to reading phrases or sentences. The student can also be taught to underline or highlight the words prior to reading the words aloud.

2.2　Oral Reading Points

Use a group point chart (see illustration) to award points for oral reading. A point is awarded to the entire group for each sentence that a student reads aloud without any errors. The chart can be posted in the classroom or on an overhead transparency so all students are aware of the points as awarded. Accompany the awarding of points with effective praise. For example, "Good job, Janet. You read the whole sentence without any errors. You earned another point for the group!" Group points can be exchanged for other reinforcers selected by the students.

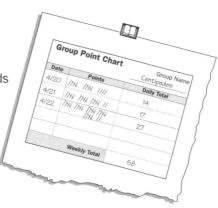

Note: Points can be awarded for other behaviors like students knowing their place when it is their turn to read, reading with expression, following along, not blurting out, etc.

2.3　Stop and Switch

Divide the class into two or more teams. (Rows or tables can also constitute teams.) Students are assigned a partner at the beginning of a practice activity. The pairs or dyads also participate on one of the teams. At any time while students are working on the practice assignment the teacher can call out, "Stop and switch!" Students immediately trade papers with their partner for checking. The teacher can randomly select specific problems for checking, or all of the items can be checked from the point where the last switch occurred. Accuracy points can be written in the margin of the assignment. Partners can add their accuracy points together for a combined total. The total number of points for the partners are then reported/recorded toward their team score. Each member of the winning team of the day can receive a special reward such as a reduced homework certificate, free time activity, etc.

Team 1	M	T	W	Th	F	Total	Team 2	M	T	W	Th	F	Total
Billy & Sarah	4	9					Jeffrey & Alisha	3	7				
Janet & Frank	6	8					Jerome & Alex	10	6				
Eunice & Larry	8	2					Jennifer & Gabriel	10	4				
Team Total:							**Team Total:**						

2.4 Self-Check and Count

Provide students with an answer key upon completion of the practice assignment. Teach the students how to check and count their own work by circling or marking every component of their answer that matches the answer key, rather than looking at only the final answer. By counting each component of the answer, students are reinforced for partially correct answers and are provided with corrective feedback.

```
  ¹ ₄
    25
  x 38
   200
    75
   950
```

EXAMPLES

- In counting math answers, every correct digit written should be given a count, along with counts for correct alignment, drawing lines, and other critical elements necessary for solving the problem. In the following example, there could be a possible correct count of 12, (8 digits, 2 numbers carried, 1 alignment, and 1 line above the answer) when counting digits, alignment, carried numbers, and the line.

- In counting spelling, the student can be taught to count every correct letter written in sequence. For instance, the following demonstrates how students could self-check their spelling of "black." For instance, the student wrote blak for black: count of three correct letters in sequence (b-l-a), count of one error (left the 'c' out altogether). If the student wrote blakc for black: count of three correct letters in sequence (b-l-a), count of two errors ('k' and 'c' are out of sequence).

- In checking handwriting, counts could be given for correct formation of each letter, correct slant of each letter, correct size on line for each letter, and correct ending stroke.

purple

• In checking writing, counts could be given for each word written, punctuation mark, capital letter, complete sentence, etc.

A recording sheet can be used for corrects and errors. Points can then be awarded for correct answers. Points can be subtracted for incorrect responses.

Self-Check and Count

Date	Corrects	−	Errors	= Total Points
5/1	63	−	4	= 59

2.5   Magic Pens

Before practice assignments are handed out, use an invisible ink Transformer Pen and randomly draw stars close to where the answers will be written. Start by marking one or two stars for every five problems. Tell the students that several items are marked with the invisible ink pen and if they have written a correct answer on one of those items, they will earn special rewards.

After the students complete the entire assignment, a designated portion of the assignment, or have been working for a specified time period, have them use one of the Transformer Pens and mark over their answers. If a star shows through **and** the answer is correct, then an additional reward is provided (points, free time minutes, lottery tickets, etc.). Be sure to select items that are reinforcing to the student. Since the student does not know ahead of time where the stars have been placed on the practice assignment, there is added incentive for the student to complete all of the problems carefully and accurately. This technique can be combined with the Mystery Motivator, Wild Card Spinner, and Menu Card under T-3. Transformer Pens are available at teacher's supply stores, art supply stores, and many discount chains.

G2: What can I do about the students who make careless errors when completing practice/seatwork activities?

3.1 Change the Channel

If students are required to write answers to questions after reading the material, try using different input or output channels for completing the assignment.

EXAMPLES

- Have the students **read** the material and **say** the answers aloud.
- Have the students **listen** to the material and **say** the answers aloud.
- Have the students **read** the material and **mark** the answers.
- Have the students **listen** to the material and **mark** the answers.
- Have the students **listen** to the material and **write** the questions.
- Have the students **listen** to the material and **say** the questions aloud.

This is an accelerated version of the Change the Channel technique discussed in G1.12. Refer to this earlier version for more in depth ideas.

3.2 Page Numbers

After reading or listening to the questions, ask the students to locate and write down **page** and **paragraph** numbers where the information related to the question can be found. Students would not be required to write answers to the questions, but rather **locate information**.

3.3 Questions First

Provide the students with the **questions** related to the reading selection **prior** to the actual reading. The questions can also reference page numbers where the information that includes the answer can be found. Read the questions to the students or have them read to themselves. Ask each student to restate the question. Next, have the students read the first section of material, stopping at the end of the pages indicated for question one. After the students answer question one, have them go on to repeat the procedure for the remaining questions.

3.4   Question/Instruction Repeat

Students who have difficulty answering questions may not **understand** the question or the instructions. Check for understanding by having each student read the question/ instruction aloud. Then, ask students to repeat or restate the information in their **own words**. Or, the students could be asked to rewrite the question or the instructions in their own words.

3.5   Listen, Write, Listen, Say

The following procedure is a series of steps to enhance comprehension. It is important to be consistent in using this format so that students learn a pattern for responding.

Step 1: The teacher begins by **reading a question** related to the information contained in a short paragraph.

Step 2: Then, the teacher **reads the paragraph** to the students.

Step 3: Next, the teacher **reads the question** again to the students and waits for a few seconds. Do not allow answers to be blurted. This is silent time for the students to think of the answer.

Step 4: Then, the teacher **gives the answer** to the question. Demonstrate this procedure several times with a variety of different paragraphs.

Step 5: Next, the teacher **reads the same question** as used in the above activity for one of the paragraphs.

Step 6: Instruct the students to **write their answer** and wait until students have made a response.

Step 7: The teacher then **gives the correct answer.**

Repeat this procedure with the remaining questions. The teacher can also repeat the procedure as often as needed for each paragraph or ask for verbal group response.

Source: Adapted from Buchanan, 1994.

3.6   Key Words

Identifying and defining key words from students' practice assignments is a useful strategy for helping students to understand the importance of vocabulary/definitions.

Step 1: Write the definitions for the vocabulary words on index cards. Count up the number of words in the definition and write it on the card. (If the word is igloo and the definition is "a house made of ice blocks," the definition would have a total of six possible points.)

Step 2: Divide the class into two teams. A representative from each team comes to the front of the room. One of the vocabulary cards is jointly chosen to begin the game.

Step 3: The person from team A begins by telling both teams the number of words in the definition, followed by a **key word** in the definition. (i.e., "There are six words in this definition. The first key word is ice.") Team A members discuss among themselves and then try to determine the vocabulary word based on the clue. A designated spokesperson gives the vocabulary word.

Step 4: If Team A identifies the word correctly, they are awarded the total number of points (six) for the definition. If Team A does not identify the word correctly, the player from Team B provides their team with a new key word clue (i.e., "The next key word is house."). Team B now has the opportunity to respond.

Step 5: If Team B responds correctly, they are awarded five points (a decrease of one). If they do not respond correctly, the play reverts to Team A. Another key word is given and the points awarded are once again decreased by one.

Step 6: Play continues until the vocabulary word is identified. Two new team members choose the next vocabulary word and follow the same procedures.

Step 7: The winning team is the one with the most points after all words have been presented.

igloo	a house made of ice blocks. **6**

Source: Schumaker, Deshler, Alley, & Warner, 1983.

3.7   I am Ready to Find Out

Provide the student with the "I am Ready to Find Out" index card prior to reading the selection. Instruct the student to complete who/what/where/when questions they want answered. For instance: "Who is the story about?"; "What happened to the main character?"; or "What is the sequence of events?" The answer to the question can be written in the space below the question. Students then complete the card by writing the corresponding page number that contains the answer to the question.

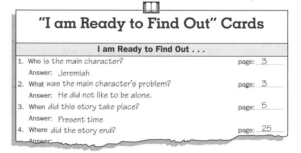

3.8   What is the Main Idea?

One technique to develop students' reading comprehension is to help them identify the main idea within a selected text.

Step 1: Tell students that the **main idea** in a passage is **a sentence** that tells about the **whole passage**.

Step 2: Read aloud to the students a short passage and then tell them in a complete sentence what the main idea is.

Step 3: Then state, "This is the main idea because it tells about the whole passage."

Step 4: Read another short passage and tell students one detail about the passage. Next say, "This is not the main idea because it does not tell about the whole passage. It only tells about one part of the whole passage."

Step 5: Repeat this modeling procedure with at least three to six other short passages using examples and nonexamples.

Step 6: Then read a short passage and tell students a detail **or** the main idea and ask, "Is this the main idea?" Wait for a group response of yes or no. Then ask, "Why?" Call on individual students or the entire group to respond with statements such as "Because it only tells about the whole passage," or "Because it only tells about only one part of the whole passage."

> **Note:** The sentence that tells about the whole passage does not necessarily appear verbatim in the passage.

3.9 Mark and Say Main Idea

This technique will work best in conjunction with What is the Main idea? as described in G3.8. Give students a card or piece of paper and read a paragraph to them. Tell students to put a mark on an index card when they think they can identify the main idea. After students have made a mark, such as an 'M,' the teacher states the main idea. Then the teacher asks the students to repeat the main idea in unison or calls on individual students to repeat the main idea. Repeat this procedure with several other short paragraphs. Later, the teacher can drop the modeling step and ask students to give the main idea after reading short passages.

3.10 Answer Experts

Assign students to "home" groups of four or five. The number of students in a group should be the same as the number of questions to be answered. Each student in the group is assigned one question related to the reading selection to answer. After reading or listening to the selection, students move to "expert" groups, joining students from the other groups who have been assigned the same question. The expert groups answer their question and write notes on an index card (see illustration). Students then return to their home group and share the answer to their question with the entire group. All students in the home group are then responsible for answering all the questions.

3.11 Add It Up

Students are taught to fill out the Add It Up organizer to arrive at the main idea. This organizer can be completed while reading aloud, silently, or just listening to a passage. Details can also be written in the boxes after the reading of the passage.

3.12 Step-by-Step

Students are taught to fill out the Step-by-Step diagram as a way to visually illustrate events in a story or passage. Have the students summarize the events of the selection by filling in the sequential squares. They can focus on chronology, character setting, or changes that occur during the passage. This can be completed while reading aloud, silently, or just listening to a passage. The diagram can also be completed after the reading of the passage.

3.13 Overlapping Circles

Overlapping circles can be used to record qualities that are shared by two (or more) entities (i.e., characters) as well as qualities that are unique to each entity. As with Add It Up and Step-by-Step, the circles can be labeled and completed while reading aloud, silently, or just listening to a passage. The diagram can also be completed after the reading of the passage. Use whichever method is better suited to the concepts being compared.

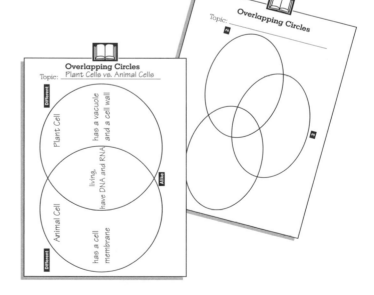

3.14 Cause/Effect

Some reading material may be visually illustrated by identifying causes and effects. See the illustration for diagrams that may be used for illustrating cause/effect, or cause/effect/after effect. The teacher could identif a cause and the students could complete the other boxes.

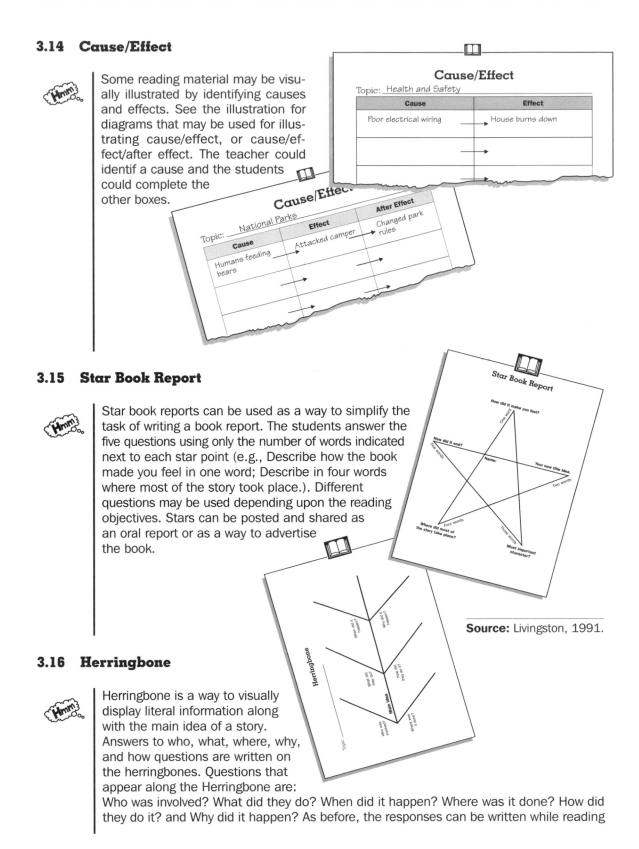

Cause/Effect

Topic: Health and Safety

Cause	Effect
Poor electrical wiring	→ House burns down
	→

Cause/Effec

Topic: National Parks

Cause	Effect	After Effect
Humans feeding bears	→ Attacked camper	→ Changed park rules
	→	→
	→	

3.15 Star Book Report

Star book reports can be used as a way to simplify the task of writing a book report. The students answer the five questions using only the number of words indicated next to each star point (e.g., Describe how the book made you feel in one word; Describe in four words where most of the story took place.). Different questions may be used depending upon the reading objectives. Stars can be posted and shared as an oral report or as a way to advertise the book.

Source: Livingston, 1991.

3.16 Herringbone

Herringbone is a way to visually display literal information along with the main idea of a story. Answers to who, what, where, why, and how questions are written on the herringbones. Questions that appear along the Herringbone are: Who was involved? What did they do? When did it happen? Where was it done? How did they do it? and Why did it happen? As before, the responses can be written while reading aloud, silently, or just listening to a passage. The diagram can also be completed after the reading of the passage.

3.17 Comprehension Wheels

Comprehension wheels are used before reading a story or passage and are completed during or after the reading of the story. The story or passage topic is written in the center circle (e.g., whales). Students are then asked to generate questions they would like answered about the topic. These are then written separately on the spokes of the Comprehension Wheel. Prompts can be provided to help students generate questions, such as "Think of a 'what' or 'who' question." The story or passage is read, and the students record the answers into the spaces between spokes. (Some questions may not be answered through reading the story and can be researched using other materials.)

Paragraphs can be written using the information on the wheel. Questions can be numbered to assist students in sequencing the information on the wheel. Topic and main idea sentences can also be inserted. Paragraphs that result from the Comprehension Wheels can be traded and edited among students.

3.18 Story Charts

Story charts are a way to visually record the information in a story, chapter, or passage. The responses can be written while reading aloud, silently, or just listening to a passage. Primary information in each column can be expanded to include other descriptive information.

Story Charts

Topic: _Studying Abroad_

Who?	Did What?	Said/Thought?	Where?	When?	Why?
• child/ Erica • only child, 16 years old	• went to far away university to learn Spanish • anxious, scared	• I'm excited and afraid • anxious, scared	• Madrid, Spain • 100°	• summer of '93	• applied and awarded a scholarship

In the Who? column, primary information might include the characters and their names. Expanded information can include words that describe the characters. In the Did What? column, primary information might include actions and events from the passage. Expanded information can include words describing the actions and events from the pasage. In the Said/Thought column, primary information might include words spoken or thought by a character. Expanded information can include words which describe how the information was spoken.

Know/Do Not Know

Topic:

Know	Do Not Know

3.19 Know/Do Not Know

Students can be taught to use the Know/Do Not Know format while they are reading stories or passages. They record what they think is being said in the

Know column and vocabulary words that are unknown or prevent their understanding of the material in the Do Not Know column. Other activities for teaching vocabulary can be used with the unknown words, such as Practice Sheets/Cards G3.21 and ideas found in T5 and T7.

3.20 Comprehension Outlines

A generic outline can be used as an alternative for acquiring information about a passage. Additional prompts (as shown in Version One) can be added to assist students who need more clues to complete the outline. Version Two would require students to write more in depth information.

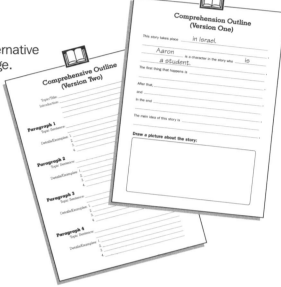

3.21 Practice Sheets/Cards

As another alternative to answering comprehension questions, students can make their own practice sheets or cards to assist in mastering the critical vocabulary and concepts. Practice sheets or cards can be used in practically any content area to facilitate comprehension and understanding.

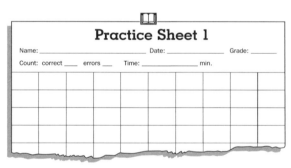

To develop and use practice sheets:

Use a blank formatted sheet copied on both sides of the page (see illustration). Five to eight different items (i.e. vocabulary words and definitions for a section of reading material) are selected for use on one practice sheet. The items are written, one per box, and repeated randomly at least two to three times on the page. The corresponding answers/definitions are written on the back side of the practice sheet in matching positions. With a partner, students practice the information during two-minute timed drills. Student A shows the vocabulary side of the page to Student B. Student B pronounces the word and then states the definition. Student A (who is looking at the answer side of the sheet) checks and gives

feedback to Student B. After two minutes, partners switch roles. Student B shows the vocabulary side of the page to Student A and the process is repeated.

To develop and use practice cards:

Students make their own index cards for critical vocabulary and concepts. On one side of the card the student writes the key concept or vocabulary word. On the back side of the card the student writes the key points associated with the concept or the definition. Students then practice by looking at the information on one side of the card and

Practice Sheet 3

Name: _____ Date: _____ Grade: _____

Count: correct _____ errors _____ Time: _____ min.

stating what is on the reverse side of the card. The student then looks at the reverse side of the card to check their answer. Students use only five to eight different cards at a time, during a two-minute timed drill. This allows students to go through the stack of cards

at least two to three times during the practice session. This activity can also be conducted with partners. One partner shows one side of the card to the partner and is able to check the answer with the information that appears of the back side of the card.

Source: Lovitt et al., 1992.

3.22 Stop and Think

Stop and Think is a strategy that allows students to think about what they are reading while they are reading or while they are listening to information. Students are taught to stop at designated points (such as after each paragraph) and ask questions or make notations about the material. Notations and marks can be made on the actual material or students can use a format with prompts to record information (see illustration). The Stop and Think format should include prompts which promote a broad based understanding of the written materials. Students should be able to record impressions, disagreements, challenges, affirmations, and expansions in their own terms.

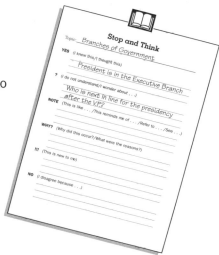

G3: What can I do about the students who do not comprehend and/or respond to written material during practice/seatwork activities?

3.23   Students Ask Questions

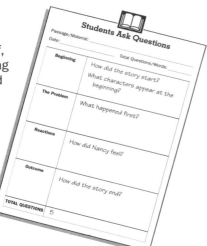

Students Ask Questions requires students to think of, then write down comprehension questions concerning what they have read. These steps should be followed after the students listen to or read information.

Step 1:   Students are given a five-minute timing to write questions pertaining to selected categories such as the ones listed in the illustration. Students should be encouraged to write one question in each category before writing multiple questions in a category. The categories can be changed depending upon the teaching objectives and the subject matter.

Step 2:   Students then count the number of questions written or the total number of words written in the questions.

Step 3:   Students then record the number of questions or the number of words on a chart or graph.

Step 4:   Students try to improve their question and word writing score the next time a Students Ask Questions timing is administered.

Alternate categories could include characters, setting, problem, and solution.

Source: Lovitt et al., 1992.

3.24   Study Guides (Prompts)

A study guide with page numbers can be used to assist students in locating answers to questions in textbooks. Other prompts can be incorporated into the study guide format depending upon the needs of the student. Study guides can be completed by an individual student, partners, or in cooperative learning groups.

Study Guide—Chapter 11
Worms

1.   How many roundworm species have been identified?   _____

2.   In roundworms, hydrostatic pressure is antagonistic to the   _____

3.   Most roundworms are monoecious. T or F   _____

4.   Name two body systems that are missing in roundworms.   _____

5.   Roundworms are in what phylum?   _____

6.   Name the roundworm parasite that:
   a.   burrows through the bottoms of the feet   _____
   b.   causes itching   _____
   c.   is obtained by ingesting undercooked pork   _____
   d.   is often found in all members of a family   _____
   e.   its eggs are killed by sunlight and high temperatures   _____
   f.   causes elephantiasis   _____

G3: What can I do about the students who do not comprehend and/or respond to written material during practice/seatwork activities?

3.25 Graphic Organizers

 Visual-spatial maps or graphic organizers may be appropriate aids, depending on the comprehension task that is required of the students. The use of graphic organizers should be introduced, modeled, and demonstrated for the students before use as a comprehension activity or for answering questions. After instruction, the organizers can be completed by an individual student, partners, or in a cooperative group setting. The teacher should determine if a **blank copy** of the organizer should be used (see illustration), a **partially completed version** which includes some of the information, or a **complete copy** which contains all of the information. Additionally, an appropriate format should be selected based upon the practice activity and the objective.

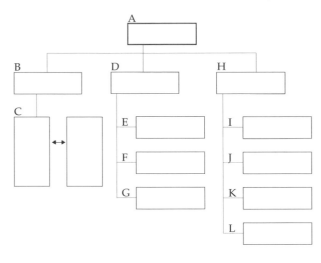

Source: Lovitt et al., 1992.

3.26 SR.I.SRV (Scanning)

 SR.I.SRV is a six-step scanning for information strategy. SR.I.SRV is ideal for answering questions at the end of a chapter or other questions related to printed material. Scanning does not require the student to read all of the information.

Step 1: **S**urvey the written material. Look for:
    a. Title
    b. Headings/subheadings
    c. Stand-out words (e.g., bold faced, italicized, underlined, etc.)

Step 2: **R**ead the question that needs to be answered.

Step 3: **I**dentify key words in the question and determine what you are to do.

Step 4: **S**earch the written material for the key word(s).

Step 5: **R**ead the sentences that fall before and after the key word(s) and answer the question.

Step 6: **V**erify your answer.

Students are taught through teacher modeling and example what each step entails and how to utilize them. Students easily remember this strategy as "Sir I Serve." Students,

G3: What can I do about the students who do not comprehend and/or respond to written material during practice/seatwork activities?

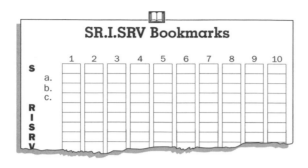

when prompted, will use this strategy to acquire critical information from written material. The illustration shows a bookmark that can be laminated for students as a way to remember the steps and self-monitor their use of the strategy. Students check a box under the question number after using the step in the strategy.

Source: Lovitt et al., 1992.

3.27 SQ3R Worksheets

SQ3R Worksheets is a five step study skill designed to improve reading comprehension. Students are first taught each of the steps in the strategy through teacher modeling and examples. During structured practice activities the worksheet shown in the illustration can be used to assist students in more purposeful reading.

Step 1: **Survey:** The students look over the entire written selection before reading it. Items that should be surveyed include the title, subheadings, pictures, charts, graphs, stand-out words (bold, italic, etc.), bullets, summary section, and any questions at the end of the selection.

Step 2: **Question:** The students formulate questions that the selection is likely to answer. For example, if the title of the selection is *Events That Shaped the Revolution*, students might ask, "What happened to help start the American Revolution?" All questions should be written down on the worksheet.

Step 3: **Read:** The students read (or listen to) the selection while looking for the answers to the formulated questions. Key words or notes could be written next to each question to assist in recall.

Step 4: **Recite:** After the selection has been read, the students should recite or write the answers to the questions. If the questions cannot be answered, the selection can be read again or another resource may be used to locate the answer.

Step 5: Review: Sometime later, and always before a test on the material, the reader should go back over the worksheet questions and check for retention.

Source: Lovitt et al., 1992.

4.1 Cooperation Keys

Teach the entire class what the key skills of cooperation **look** and **sound** like. Some of the skills required in order to work with others are:

Attentive Listening: With full attention and nonverbal encouragement.

Put Ups and Appreciation: Prohibit the exchange of put downs and teach words of praise and encouragement.

The Right to Pass: This does not mean lack of participation, but an option to choose when to participate.

Confidentiality: No names or gossip about group work.

4.2 Partner Board

A partner board, such as the one illustrated, is displayed in the classroom for the purpose of recognizing the students that are working well together. The teacher also carries around a cooperative partner book while students are working together. Each student's name is listed in the book. As the teacher is observing the student's activities, a check is placed next to his or her name to recognize cooperation. The students with the highest number of checks at the end of the activity are given additional recognition by having their names displayed on the partner board.

PARTNER BOARD		
Sharing		
Shelly		**Effort** Vivian
Campbell		
Leroy		
Cooperation Frank		
Mary		

4.3   Step Out

Designate a place in the classroom where students go to step out of the group if they are not using the appropriate cooperative skills for working in a group. The teacher determines and announces ahead of time the criteria for being moved to the step out area such as the length of stay, expected behavior during the step out time period, and the reentry procedures. The teacher signals the student if it is necessary for them to step out. If a student steps out more than once during an activity, additional consequences can be given.

4.4   Team Skills

Step 1: Students are first assigned an individual task to accomplish. This could be a specific portion of a state report, a set of math problems, or individual thoughts and important learnings from a text.

Step 2: The students are assigned a group product that incorporates the individual task; an entire state report, an entire math assignment, or a compilation of individual learnings in order of importance.

Step 3: It is explained to the students that they are expected to work in groups to produce the final product while practicing specific teamwork skills. Some examples of team skills include: taking turns, listening to others, disagreeing appropriately, keeping everyone involved, and contributing to group work.

Step 4: The teacher chooses one or two specific team skills for the groups to work on and carefully defines what each looks and sounds like. In addition, students are given a specific timeline for completing the group project.

Step 5: After completion of the final product, the teacher debriefs with the groups to discuss and evaluate their use of the team skills. (See G4.6 and G4.8 for additional ideas.) Some questions to use might include: How did you use the skills in your group? How often did the group members use the skill? How did you feel using the skill? What might you change for the next time? How would you rate your own use of the skill?

Step 6: Questionnaires or surveys can be used as well as group discussion. Feedback should be given to the groups by the teacher as well as by the team members.

Step 7: The teacher can also have students write down the skills they used and their goal for improvement in a teamwork skills notebook. These goals can be referred to from time to time and progress can be noted by the teacher or the group.

Step 8: Time should also be spent reviewing the academic task in order to further the group's understanding of the subject matter.

4.5   Role Cards

Prior to having students work with others, assign specific roles for each student to perform in the group. Provide students with specific behavioral descriptions for each role.

G4: What can I do about the students who do not work cooperatively, or rely on others to do the practice/seatwork activities?

Some roles that can be assigned are:

Summarizer/Checker—   Ensures that everyone in the group understands the information.

Research/Runner—   Retrieves the necessary materials for the group and is the communication link with other groups and the teacher.

Recorder/Writer—   Writes down the group's conclusions and edits the final copy.

Encourager—   Reinforces group members' contributions.

Observer—   Keeps track of the group's performance and how well everyone is collaborating.

Quiet Captain—   Makes sure the group does not disturb others.

The Gatekeeper—   Keeps everyone participating and makes sure that no one person is dominating the group.

Other names can be assigned to these roles to fit the age level of the students and content being taught. For instance:

MATH GROUP ROLES

Calculator—   Verifies work on calculator.

Analyst—   Determines which strategies the group should use.

Bookkeeper—   Verifies final work and records time spent.

Inventory Controller—   Keeps track of material and supplies.

NOVEL DISCUSSION GROUP ROLES

Discussion Leader—   Prepares and leads questions with the group.

Vocabulary Enricher—   Selects enrichment questions for review.

Literary Illuminary—   Reads critical passages and information.

Agent—   Retrieves materials and supplies and is the communication link with the teacher.

SCIENCE GROUP ROLES

Scientist—   Observes group progress and keeps track of time.

Researcher—   Provides guidelines for the group to follow.

Observer—   Records information about the lesson and/or the group.

Lab Technician—   Sets up materials and equipment the group is to use.

SOCIAL STUDIES GROUP ROLES

Presiding Officer—   Facilitates what goes on in the group.

Secretary—   Records information that is processed by the group.

Parliamentarian—   Observes group progress with the topic.

Sergeant at Arms—   Keeps time, retrieves supplies, communication link with
                                              the teacher.

PRIMARY GROUP ROLES

Happy Talker—   Makes positive comments about student contributions.

Turn Taker—   Makes sure everyone is involved and has their turn at par-
                                              ticipating.

Helper—   Retrieves materials and is communication link with the
                                              teacher.

Source: Johnson et al., 1987.

4.6 Reflection Cards

After group work, have students complete individual
and/or group written evaluations related to the skill(s)
while working with one another. This type of evaluation requires a high level of trust among students
and some training in feedback procedures. Reflec-
tions to include are: (1) Name one thing you learned
about working with others; and (2) What is one skill
you could improve upon? If a particular student is
having a difficult time, have the individual student
fill out an evaluation and process the information with the teacher.

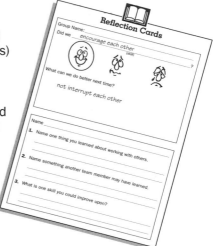

4.7 Assignment Co-Op

Assign students into groups of three or four. Divide up the
assignment so each person of the group is responsible for completing
only a portion of the assignment. Establish time frames for completion and allow students
to work within the group while completing their individual portions. When completed, each
student in the group must share the information they were responsible for with the entire
group. A group product can be compiled using each member's information. Tests should be
administered individually and bonus points should be awarded to teams whose members all
score above a specified grade. The purpose of the bonus point is to encourage group work,
sharing of information, and cooperation.

G4: What can I do about the students who do not work cooperatively, or rely on others to do the practice/seatwork activities?

4.8   Processing

Processing is discussing, reflecting, and evaluating with students how partners or groups functioned during an activity. Classwide processing can include feedback from observations made by the teacher and some observations from members of the class. Names should not be used when processing with the whole group, but the feedback should be as specific as possible. Groups that are new to processing, often need an agenda, including specific questions each group must address. A simple agenda might include: Name two things the group/dyad did well and one thing they need to do even better. Group processing should focus on member's contributions to the learning along with questions regarding the maintenance of effective working relationships among partners/groups. Some possible questions for group processing follow.

EXAMPLES

- What did you do that helped your team work together?
- What could you change in order to improve next time?
- How is your team working as a group?
- What would you do differently next time?
- How did you feel about your group?
- What did you notice that might help the team?
- What was the best thing that happened to your group?
- What changes would make your group even more successful?

Processing can be done on an individual basis by having students fill out a simple rating scale regarding their own performance. Each student can then share the self-rating with their partners by explaining why they rated themselves as they did and what they could do next time to improve.

EXAMPLES

- **How well did you check to make sure your partners understood the material you presented?**

- **How well did you share supplies with your group?**

G4: What can I do about the students who do not work cooperatively, or rely on others to do the practice/seatwork activities?

4.9   Classwide Peer Tutoring

Classwide peer tutoring is a structured tutoring situation where students practice material but also earn rewards and bonus points for working cooperatively with others. The following steps will help you set up classwide peer tutoring in the classroom.

Step 1:   **Divide the class into two teams.** Students can be randomly assigned to teams or the teacher may make team assignments. Teams should choose a team name, color, or logo.

Step 2:   **Assign students to dyads (tutoring pairs).** Students can be randomly assigned or the teacher may want to make assignments based on individual needs. These dyads should be heterogeneous.

Step 3:   **Train the dyads to conduct tutoring session.** Carefully demonstrate and model the tutoring procedure described in this section. Students also need to be taught to use an individual scorecard (see illustration) to keep track of correct and error responses. Students should practice the procedure prior to implementation.

Students are assigned as tutor and tutee. The tutor begins by asking the tutee the designated questions in the content area. After 15 minutes or so, the partners switch and the student who responded the first time, now asks the questions. Bonus points are awarded by the teacher who is circulating the room during the tutoring sessions. These points are given for social behaviors that have been predetermined by the teacher and announced to the class. Bonus points are recorded on the dyad's scorecard to help reinforce the tutoring procedure and working cooperatively.

Step 4:   **Total the points from the tutoring session.** The students in each dyad add the points earned from the questions and the bonus points together for a daily total.

Step 5:   **Record the dyad point totals on a game chart.** The total scores for each dyad are collected by the teacher, either by having students call out their total or through an individual student recorder. Since these scores are combined for each dyad the chance of embarrassment is greatly reduced and students work cooperatively to raise their combined scores. Dyads with the highest daily score can be recognized.

Step 6:   **Recognize the winning team of the week.** After all dyad scores are totaled by team, the team with the highest total score is the winning team for the week. Some form of recognition should be given to this team. Ideas for reinforcement could be: Posting results on a class or school bulletin board, printing results in a weekly newsletter, providing all team members with achievement certificates, notes home to parents, or rewards that may be tied into the classroom management system.

Step 7:   **Assess student performance on material practiced by tutors.** Quizzes or some other type of evaluation should be administered individually on a regular basis to determine student growth on the practiced material.

G4: What can I do about the students who do not work cooperatively, or rely on others to do the practice/seatwork activities?

Scorecard

Step 1: A scorecard can have any number of items. This example is based on 15 items.

Step 2: A plus (+) or minus (-) is recorded for each item.

Step 3: If no errors occur during round one, then 25 points are awarded.

Scoring Errors

Step 1: If one or more errors occur during the first round, then the student goes to the second round.

Step 2: In the second round, only the missed items from round one are presented and responded to.

Step 3: If the student responds correctly to the items in round two, then 20 points are awarded.

Step 4: If an error occurs in round two, then the student goes to round three (15 points) or round four (15 points), if necessary.

Classwide Score Sheet

Step 1: Total the points from tutoring sessions.

Step 2: Dyads total daily round points and bonus points for each dyad from their individual scorecards.

Step 3: Dyads record them on a classwide score sheet posted in the classroom.

Source: Lovitt et al., 1992.

STUDENT SCORECARD				
Tutoring Items	Round 1 (25)	Round 2 (20)	Round 3 (15)	Round 4 (15)
1.				15
2.		20		
3.			15	
4.	25			
5.	25			
6.				
7.				
8.				
9.				
10.				
11.				
12.				
13.				
14.				
15.				
Round				
Bonus				
TOTAL				

CLASSWIDE SCORE SHEET					
Dyad Points	M	T	W	TH	F
1. Tutoring	48				
Quiz					
2. Tutoring	39				
Quiz					
3. Tutoring	54				
Quiz					
4. Tutoring	35				
Quiz					
5. Tutoring					
Quiz					
6. Tutoring					
Quiz					
7. Tutoring					
Quiz					
8. Tutoring					
Quiz					
9. Tutoring					
Quiz					
10. Tutoring					
Quiz					
TOTAL					
WEEKLY TOTAL					

G4: What can I do about the students who do not work cooperatively, or rely on others to do the practice/seatwork activities?

4.10   Team-Building Exercises

Prior to placing students with partners or in groups, have the entire class participate in activities that promote belonging and trust. If a student does not feel included in a classroom, he or she will create his or her own inclusion by grabbing influence (attracting attention, creating controversy, demanding power, or taking control). Examples of some team-building exercises are listed below.

EXAMPLES

- **Wishful Thinking**

  Students sit in a circle. Each person makes a brief statement beginning with "I wish . . . ." There is no discussion during the activity and statements can be related to personal life, feelings about school, the group, friends, etc. After everyone has had a chance to make a statement, debrief with questions such as: Do we share common wishes? How did you feel? Did others listen to you? How did you know they listened to you?

- **Something Good**

  Students sit in a circle. Each person shares one positive experience that happened during the past week with no discussion occurring until all have shared. Ask follow-up questions such as: Were there any similarities about the good things shared? When was the last time you told someone about a positive experience? Was it hard to think of something good to share?

- **Build a Better Bathtub**

  Break students into small groups of three or five. Have each group appoint a recorder. (Younger groups can use an aide or older student as recorder.) Provide groups with the rules for brainstorming:

  D (defer judgment)
  O (off-beat, original)
  V (vast number of ideas)
  E (expand, elaborate on other's ideas)

  Tell groups they have five minutes to call out and write down as many ideas as possible on the subject: How could we design a better bathtub? One that provides more enjoyment, efficiency, and comfort than ordinary tubs. The recorder jots down all ideas. Stop the brainstorming after five minutes and ask each recorder to read the list. Lead the applause after each group's presentation.

  After, the teacher asks questions such as: Are many heads better than one in producing a wide range of ideas? What would have happened if we had judged, commented, or discussed ideas as they were being offered? Did each group have fun?

  Source: Gibbs, 1987.

G4: What can I do about the students who do not work cooperatively, or rely on others to do the practice/seatwork activities?

5.1 Huddle

Encourage students to huddle with a partner or team to compare answers, ideas, or comments before contributing the information individually. A more structured version of this technique is Heads Together found in T8.6.

5.2 Write and Speak

Prior to the discussion, have students respond to open-ended questions related to the topic. Have students write down their thoughts and ideas on paper first, then share their ideas with one other person before being asked to contribute.

5.3 Signals

Set up a signal or cue ahead of time to let students know when they will be expected to contribute information. A brief consultation about what will take place during the discussion and examples of ideas or comments for contribution will give the student additional preparation time.

5.4 Contribution Points

Keep track of student contributions with the use of a contribution checklist or board. Award points for the number or type of contributions made (facts, opinions, additional ideas, or insights). Points can be tallied for individual rewards or they can be added into each student's participation grade.

5.5 Contribution Chips

Put four or five students in a small discussion group. Each group member is allotted an equal number of chips he or she must use throughout the discussion. When a member contributes information, they place a chip in the middle of the table. When a student's chips run out, he or she cannot talk again until everyone in the group has contributed. Chips cannot be taken or given away by any member of the group.

Source: Kagan, 1990.

G5: What can I do about the students who do not contribute to class discussions during practice activities?

5.6   Pens in the Jar

Put four or five students in a small discussion group. Place a jar in the middle of the table with different colored pens, sticks, or markers representing each student. When a student makes a contribution, they pull their pen or marker and place it in front of them. Before that student can speak again, the other group members must make a contribution. After all members of the group have contributed, the pens are placed back in the jar and the discussion continues following the same procedure.

Source: Kagan, 1990.

5.7   Corners

The teacher writes different ideas or questions related to a specific topic on chart paper and posts them in the four corners of the classroom. When the teacher gives the signal, each student moves to one of the corners. Once in their selected corner, they pair up and discuss the reasons for their choice. After a specified time of discussion, the teacher randomly selects pairs to report their thinking to the class.

EXAMPLES

- **Volleyball skills:** Serve, bump, set, spike. (What skill would you like most to develop?)

- **Current Issues:** Poverty, drug abuse, gang violence, pollution. (If you were governor of your state, which issue would be top priority? Why?)

- **Novels/Storybooks:** Characters and events from the story. (Who was your favorite character? Which character do you think was most responsible for the dilemma? Why?)

- **Controversial Issues:** Strongly agree, disagree, agree, strongly disagree. (All students are treated fairly at our school. Why do you believe this? Defend your position.)

Source: Kagan, 1990.

5.8   Graffiti Papers

Students are placed in groups of three or four. Each group is given a sheet of butcher paper with a different topic/question printed on the top and different colored marking pens. For a specified period of time (three to five minutes), every group writes "graffiti" (words, phrases, pictures) on their particular topic. Graffiti would be the students' reactions, impressions, interpretations, or creative response to/of the topic or question. The teacher then stops the groups and has each group pass their graffiti sheet to the next group and the process repeats itself. After each group has had an opportunity to respond to every question. The papers are given to the original group and the members of that group present a brief summary of what was written by all groups.

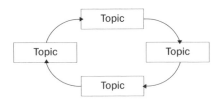

Source: Gibbs, 1987.

G5: What can I do about the students who do not contribute to class discussions during practice activities?

5.9   Inside/Outside Circle

Use the following technique as a way to involve individual students in small groups or the entire class.

Step 1:   Have students form two concentric circles, with the inside circle facing out and the outside facing in. Two or three separate circles can be formed if it is a large class. The teacher then asks the students to respond to a question related to a specific topic. Pairs of students discuss, consult, and share their ideas.

Step 2:   After students have shared their answer with the person across from them, have everyone turn right face and rotate.

Step 3:   The teacher calls, "Stop!" and the students respond to the same question again or a new question with a different partner.

Step 4:   Rotation can be one by one or random stops. Questions can also range from easy to more complex as the rotation is completed.

5.10   Making a Contribution

Describe and model the following steps for contributing to a discussion in class. Be sure students have ample opportunity for structured practice of the skill before expecting them to use it on their own. This strategy can be used along with contribution points or a contribution score board.

Step 1:   Think about the topic being discussed for one minute.

Step 2:   Signal your desire to talk by using a hand raise or another appropriate signal.

Step 3:   Look at the person or group.

Step 4:   Make a comment related to the topic.

Step 5:   Listen for a response and follow up with another comment if appropriate.

Think, then say a comment related in some way.

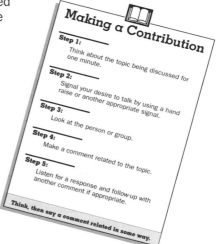

5.11   Pair Interviews

Use pair interviews at the beginning or end of a lesson to engage all students in discussion. Students are placed in groups of four and then paired off. The partners interview each other first and then reconvene with their group for a round robin. A round robin consists of each person on the team sharing in turn what they learned from the person they interviewed. The content of the interview questions can include anything. Questions that are related to the subject, but do not have one right answer are best.

G5: What can I do about the students who do not contribute to class discussions during practice activities?

EXAMPLES

Anticipatory or closure questions:

- "What do you want to learn about this topic?"
- "What experiences have you had with the information we are going to talk about?"
- "What was the most important thing you learned about this topic?"
- "When would you use this information?"
- "What would you like to know more about?"

Content specific questions:

- "How would you feel if you were Huck Finn?"
- "What math problem did you find the most difficult?"
- "If you were a scientist, how would you solve this?"
- "What would you bring if you were a pioneer traveling west?"

Source: Kagan, 1990.

5.12 Contribution Aims

After teaching students the strategy for making a contribution (see G5.10), have the students self-monitor their performance. Set aims for the number of contributions expected during the class period and have the student record the number of contributions made. Give the students tracker cards (see illustration) or have them make their own.

5.13 S.M.A.R.T.S. Review

S.M.A.R.T.S. stands for Self-Motivational and Recreational Teaching Strategies. Students are assigned to heterogeneous teams of five in order to answer the questions related to the topic of study. The student who does not often contribute to discussions could be appointed as a team captain. The teacher selects a performing team (PT) to start. All other teams become opposing teams (OT). A S.M.A.R.T.S. class score sheet is used to identify the questions and the point values that will be used during the game. The performing team begins by playing a complete round (parts one and two) of the game.

Part One:

The team captain confers with the team and selects a question from the chart. Students can choose from who/what, when/where, or how/why questions. The team must answer the question after only one minute of conferencing. Only the team captain can answer aloud. All other teams are conferencing at the same time in case the PT answers incorrectly.

If the PT answers correctly, they are awarded the predetermined point value and this is recorded on the team's score sheet by the recorder. If they are incorrect, an opposing team chosen by the teacher can give their answer and be awarded the points.

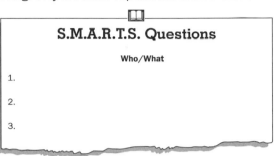

Part Two:

The PT must now answer an extended question related to the original question (i.e., spell or define a word or term). If they are correct, points are awarded to the team. If the team's answer is incorrect, then an opposing team may answer and receive the points. After completing the round of play, a new team becomes the performing team and play continues.

This game can be played in one class period or over a number of days. Teams keep track of their points and are recognized for their performance.

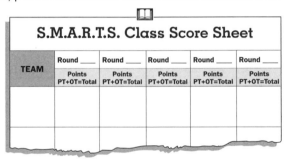

Source: Buchannan, 1989.

Independent
Practice Activities

1.1   Assignment Buddies

Assign each student in the class a buddy. Each day after giving a homework assignment, the assignment buddies check each other's assignment notebook to see if all the necessary information is written down and all the necessary materials are going home. Points can be awarded for organization and accuracy of information.

1.2   Think Out Loud

This procedure, which encourages independent thought and discovery, enables students to organize and manage by verbally repeating teacher instructions in their own words. See G1.2 for more information on getting students to "think out loud."

1.3   Mystery Motivators

This technique, previously discussed in the Teacher-Directed section of this book, can also be applied for students having problems with organizational skills. See T3.6 for more information.

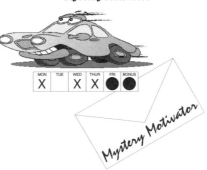
Speed Away for a Mystery Motivator

Source: Jenson et al., 1994.

1.4   Am I Working?

Use a beeper tape that sounds at random intervals. Provide the students with a card that has yes/no or happy face/sad face columns. Instruct the students that each time they hear a beep, ask themselves, Am I working? If the answer is **yes**, a mark is placed in the yes or happy face side of the card. If the student responds **no**, a mark is made on the no or sad face side of the card. At the completion of the activity, the teacher evaluates the students' performance by reviewing the cards with each student and the amount of work completed.

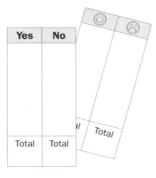

I1: What can I do about the students who do not organize or manage assignments, materials, and/or time?

Rewards and goal setting can be combined with this technique if the student needs additional motivation.

Source: Beck, 1993.

1.5   Make the GRADE

Design a Make the GRADE poster to hang in the classroom. Model examples for the students of what each of the steps in the mnemonic mean, and how they can be successful in the classroom if they use each of the steps.

Step 1: **G**et Ready. Arrive on time for class and be prepared with the necessary materials.

Step 2: **R**ecord Assignments. Use an assignment notebook to keep track of required work.

Step 3: **A**sk Questions. Get clarification if you are not sure about an assignment or activity.

Step 4: **D**esign a Plan. Come up with a plan of action for completing assignments.

Step 5: **E**valuate. How did you do? What worked or did not work in the plan you designed.

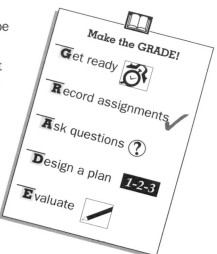

Source: Pidek, 1993.

1.6   Assignment Initials

Choose a behavior that needs to be reinforced, such as recording assignments or managing materials. The target student and the teacher each use a different colored pen for this game. When the student performs the behavior correctly, he or she is allowed to connect two dots to form one line. If the student does not follow through on the desired behavior, the teacher or parent is allowed to draw a line. Once four lines are drawn to complete a box, the student or teacher/parent places their initials in the box. At the end of the week or month, if the student has more boxes filled in, a reward may be earned.

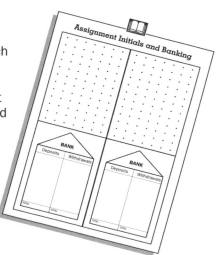

This activity can be used with students and teachers in school or students and parents at home.

Source: Pidek, 1993.

I1: What can I do about the students who do not organize or manage assignments, materials, and/or time?

1.7   Assignment Banking

Students make bank deposits or withdrawals by placing tally marks on the appropriate side of the bank. If students remember to record assignments, organize their notebooks, or manage materials, a mark is placed on the deposit side. If students do not remember, a mark is placed on the withdrawal side. If students have more marks on the deposit side at the end of the week, a reward may be earned. Weekly aims for number of deposits and withdrawals can be determined prior to implementation.

Note: The Assignment Initials and Assignment Banking appear on one form in the companion book and can be used in conjunction with one another.

1.8   Organization Cards

Give each student individual cards to track their organization skills. At the end of the class period or day, the teacher initials the students' cards in the T.I. column. At the end of the week the point total (P.T.) can be written at the bottom. Reinforce according to performance and improvement.

Did I Bring . . . ?			
	Binder	Book	Material	Teacher's Initials
Monday	✓	✓	✓	KK
Tuesday				
Wednesday				
Thursday				
Friday				
Point Total				

1.9   Assignment Log

Teach students to fill out a daily assignment log. The students fill in the subject, class assignment, and homework boxes. Materials, if necessary should be indicated by checking the Yes/No boxes. If the assignment was completed in class, the student checks the appropriate box under the done column. If the No box was checked, then the student writes in the homework assignment in the next column. Upon completion or noncompletion of homework, the student marks the appropriate box in the final Done column. Daily and/or weekly rewards can be given for completion. Yes/No totals can be figured in the bottom row. This self-monitoring technique can be combined with Transformer Pens, Wild Card Spinners, and Menu of Options Cards as described in G2.6 and T3.4.

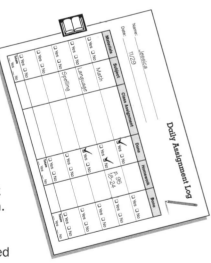

Source: Fister & Kemp, 1994.

I1: What can I do about the students who do not organize or manage assignments, materials, and/or time?

1.10 Time Management Charts

Use daily and weekly time charts to identify the varying responsibilities students have and how much time is needed for homework. Assist students in making a schedule for study and homework time. Provide students with a chart (see illustration) and have them fill in the times that are committed for sports, family time, chores etc. Help them to identify when an appropriate study time would be. Have students keep track of the time they spend daily on homework and make a visual chart so they can follow their progress.

1.11 Self-Management

Provide students with self-management cards (see illustration) that can be kept on their desks. Identify two or three specific study behaviors that are expected of the student. These could be behaviors like attentive silence, attending to answers, and using the appropriate strategy for getting the teacher's attention. Instruct the student to record these desired behaviors on their card. A drawing or photograph of the student engaged in the behaviors can also be used to illustrate the expectations. Draw exclamation points in at least two of every five blocks with the invisible ink Transformer Pen.

During independent work, set a timer or use an interval tape to sound every three minutes. Tell the students that for every three minutes of appropriate working time a block can be filled in on the study card using one Transformer Pen. If one of the invisible ink exclamation points shows through, the student earns a spin on the Wild Card Spinner (see T3.4) or another predetermined reinforcer.

1. Writing answers. ✏			
2. Asking questions. ?			
	!	!	

1.12 Parent Partners

Invite parents to come to school for an overview of the organizational strategies that will be used with their child. Obtain parental support by having parents agree to help their child become more organized at home. Information given to parents about the program/strategies used at school will provide consistency for the student in both environments. The following is a sample letter and form that can be used with parents and students when setting up organization programs.

Dear Parents,

We will be focusing on organization skills throughout the school year. Your child will need a three-ring binder, paper, pencil, eraser, ruler, and zippered pouch. The students will be expected to bring the binder and materials to each class everyday. Additional organization techniques will be added as the year progresses.

I will be inviting you to school to explain in more detail the methods, materials, and timelines for implementing the program. If you have any questions, please call me at school at _____. I am excited about this new program and look forward to working with you and your child.

Sincerely,

$\overline{}$

                                        Tear apart here
- -

I would like to be a parent partner and I agree to help my child with organization skills by providing:
   three-ring binder
   paper
   pencil
   eraser
   ruler
   zippered pouch

                          Signed_____

1.13 Assignment Notebooks

Instruct students in how to use notebooks for recording and tracking assignments. Assignment notebooks can be made or purchased in a variety of styles. If three-ring binders are used, they should include: calendars for assignment due dates; a plastic pouch for pencils, erasers, pens, paper punch, etc.; folder pockets to hold class assignments, study guides etc., loose leaf paper and spiral notebook for each class, and strategy cards for notetaking and scanning for information. (See LITES in T10.5 and SR.I.SRV in G3.26)

When notebooks are introduced into the classroom the following sections should be included: subject, assignment, due date, things to bring home, things to bring to school, special projects or long term assignments, and upcoming tests. Prior to using the assignment notebooks, demonstration, discussion, and practice should be provided on how to use them.

I1: What can I do about the students who do not organize or manage assignments, materials, and/or time?

Elementary Versions

Secondary Versions

Source: Pidek, 1991.

I1: What can I do about the students who do not organize or manage assignments, materials, and/or time?

2.1   Daily Checkout

At the end of the class period or the end of the day, have students go through a checkout list. This can be posted in the class or in assignment notebooks. Items to be checked off might include: Did I put all materials away? Are my papers turned in? What materials do I need for homework? Do I understand the work? The teacher can use the checklist as a ticket out of class, or can have students check one another's lists before starting the next activity.

Name: _____

Daily Checkout	Monday	Tuesday	Wednesday	Thursday	Friday
1. All materials away.					
2. Papers turned in.					
3. Homework materials ready.					
4. Homework instructions clear.					

2.2   Stop/Go Folders

Provide students with red and green folders, or folders labelled "stop" and "go." When students have completed an assignment, the paper goes in the stop folder so it can be handed in or corrected. If a paper is incomplete, it goes in the go folder. Work in the go folder can be finished at recess, during free time, or at another designated time. Provide students with deadlines for the work that remains in the go folder.

2.3 Home/School Talk

Arrange with parents to have students complete a home/school note each day that will be initialed by the teacher and the parent. Combine this technique with other motivation systems such as Mystery Motivators, Wild Card Spinners, or Daily Bingo.

2.4 Home/School Folders

Provide target students with folders that are sent home each day. The folders include work that has been completed in class along with assignments that need to be worked on. A log sheet (see illustration) can be attached inside the folder to track the status of assignments. Parents can be kept informed regarding assignments completed/not completed along with due dates. Points can be awarded for parent initials, work submitted, and returning the folder each day.

Home/School Log

Date	Assignment	Completed	Turned In	Parent Signature
12/24	Division	✓	✓	SH

2.5 Homework Tracking Charts

A class homework tracking chart (see illustration) can be kept by the teacher to monitor and assist in the evaluation of the students' homework performance. The name of each student is listed in the left column and the teacher simply makes a mark each time the assignment is turned in. The teacher can identify at a glance the status of each student in the class.

A student homework tracking chart can be kept by each student to assist them in self-monitoring their performance.

Homework Tracking Chart (Class)

Name	Week One	Week Two	Week Three	Week Four	Comments
Susan	/				
Karen	/				Talk to student.
Janet	///				
Bill	///				
John	///				

Homework Tracking Chart (Student)

Student: _____

Date	Used Note Book	Completed	Turned In	Comments

I2: What can I do about the students who do not complete or submit assignments?

2.6 Hit the Homework Target

Homework Target is a procedure which involves peers working together as teams to encourage homework completion.

Step 1: Divide the class into two teams. Pair up students within each team to become homework partners. Explain to students that they will work together to complete their homework target. Each pair needs one copy of the target seen in the illustration.

Step 2: Instruct students in the procedure for using the chart. On the day homework is assigned, the partners receive one point if both students write the information in their assignment notebooks. When the homework is due, the partners receive one point if both students completed the assignment and one point for turning in their assignments on time. Each point is entered as a tally mark in the corresponding day and week of the chart.

Step 3: At the end of the week, partners total their points and record them in the weekly total box. At the end of the month, the totals of all partners on each team are added together for the team score. The team with the highest score for the month is recognized. When beginning a new month, team members and partners can be rearranged.

Source: Pidek, 1991.

2.7 Homework Teams

Homework Teams is a cooperative structure where teams of three students are assigned specific responsibilities for homework completion.

Step 1: Organize students into teams of three and assign the following roles: scorekeeper, manager, and coach.

Step 2: Train the students in the responsibilities of each of the roles and explain that the responsibilities are to be carried out each day that homework is assigned. All students should know the responsibilities of their particular role.

Step 3: A daily team scorecard is used along with a team poster for each team to monitor and record their progress (see illustration). The daily team scorecard should give the students enough space to account for all the homework sheets returned. The team poster should provide the students with space to post the team's daily scores. Daily scores can be written as team total or average scores.

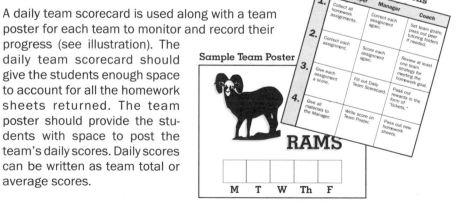

Sample Team Poster

I2: What can I do about the students who do not complete or submit assignments?

Step 4: Reinforcement can be given to both individual students or teams based on performance. Tickets or points can be awarded for meeting specific criterion set by the teacher such as all members returning assignments, perfect scores on assignments, and entire class returning assignments.

Daily Team Scorecard

Team Name: *Killer Bees*   Date: *10/23*

Homework Returned	80% or Above Correct	90% or Above Correct	100% Correct
Scott (yes) no	(yes) no	(yes) no	(yes) no
Joe (yes) no	(yes) no	(yes) no	yes (no)
Chris (yes) no	(yes) no	(yes) no	yes (no)
All returned? Team Ticket: ✓ Yes ___ No	(# of "yes"s circled = # of tickets)		All 100% Team Ticket: Yes ✓ No
Individual Tickets: _7_	Team Tickets: 0 (1) 2 (circle one)		Total Tickets: _8_

Source: Olympia, Andrews, Valum, & Jenson, 1993.

2.8   Self-Graphing Chart

Have students keep track of the number of individual problems completed during a class period or number of assignments completed during the day. Use a tracking chart (see illustration) and explain to the students that each time a problem or assignment is completed, they are to check a box on the chart. At the end of the class or day, a circle is drawn around the last checkmark indicating the total number of problems or assignments completed. If the student remembers to the turn in the assignment, bonus points can be awarded and added to the total. The circled checkmarks provide a visual display of the students performance. This technique can be combined with other reinforcement and motivation procedures.

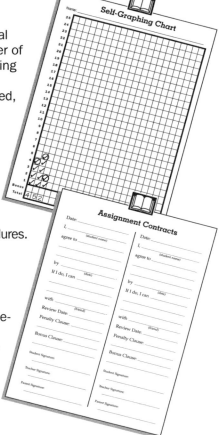

2.9   Assignment Contracts

Write a contract with students that specify what they will complete and turn in during class time or for homework. Make it a short-term contract to begin with. If students comply with the contracts, then they can be extended. Include the following information on the contract: dates, target behavior, specific reward, schedule of reinforcement, date for review of progress, signatures of everyone involved, bonus for exceptional performance, and penalties if behavior is not performed.

I2: What can I do about the students who do not complete or submit assignments?

2.10 Fill in the Dots

Provide the target student with an illustration covered with white dots. Each time the student completes an assignment, a dot is punched or filled in with a crayon or marker. When the card has been completely punched or filled in, the student receives a previously negotiated reward. If reinforcement is needed before the card is filled, Transformer Pens (see G2.5) can be used to mark several of the dots. When a student fills in a dot that has been highlighted, they receive an interim reward.

2.11 Assignment Champion Notebook

Display a notebook in the classroom that has a colorful design and cover. At the top of every page put the date and leave spaces for students to sign their name. If students complete and turn in all assignments, they become Assignment Champions and are allowed to sign the notebook that day. Add additional reinforcers for students who turn in every assignment for the week. This technique could be used as a checkout from the class or for the entire day. Give bonus points for students whose names appear a specified number of times during a unit or quarter.

2.12 How Do I Rate?

Develop recording and evaluating charts that have spaces for number of problems completed, number of problems completed correctly, and rating criteria for performance.

Step 1: Each time students finish a task, they record the total number of problems completed on their chart.

Step 2: The assignment is then graded for accuracy by the teacher or the student and the number of problems completed correctly is recorded on the chart (e.g., 8/10 reflects that the student answered eight problems correctly out of a possible ten).

Step 3: The students self-evaluate the overall performance of their completion rate.

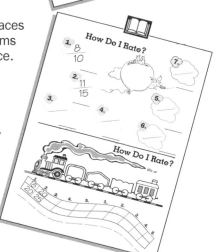

I2: What can I do about the students who do not complete or submit assignments?

The evaluation criteria is determined by the teacher, based on the student's previous completion rate. For example, if the student completed the following number of math problems last week: 28, 26, 25, 22, and 21, then the median rate of problem completion would be 25. This number would be used as the upper aim for a "1" rating and the lower point would be the median minus 20% (in this case the lower aim would be 20). If the student completes less than 20 problems, the rating is 0, if he or she completes 20-25, the rating is 1 and if he or she completes more than 25 the rating is 2.

Reinforcement can be earned if the rating is at 2 for three days in a row. The next week the median score is refigured and the student continues to record and self-evaluate until the performance is at the desired level.

Rating Chart	
21	20% of 25 = 5
22	Median (25) minus 5 = 20
(25) Median (becomes upper aim for the next week.)	20 (becomes the lower aim for the next week.)
26	
28	

Rating Scale for Example		
Below 20	=	0
21-25	=	1 pt.
Above 25	=	2 pts.

Source: Hughes et al., 1988.

3.1   I am Working/I Need Help Sign

The I am Working/I Need Help Sign consists of a laminated 3" x 5" card (or larger) taped to the front edge of the students desk. The card is attached with masking tape or strapping tape so that it can be flipped back and forth to lay on top of the student's desk or hang off the side of the desk. One side of the card is red and has the words "I Need Help." The other side of the card is green and has the words "I am Working."

During independent work time the green side of the card is facing toward the student, resting on the desk so that the sign faces the student. If help is needed, the student is instructed to flip the card over so that the red side is hanging off the edge of the desk and the words "I Need Help" are visible. The teacher can easily scan the classroom to determine which students need help by noticing the position of the red or green side of the card. After the help has been given, the card is flipped back on top of the student's desk so that the green side is showing.

A grid of boxes can be added to the green side of the card. As the teacher moves around the classroom, marks can be made in the boxes to reinforce the student for independent working behaviors, using appropriate procedures for getting the teacher's attention, etc.

3.2   Ask Three Before Me

Teach students to ask three other students for assistance before asking the teacher when they need help on independent work. Before using this procedure, demonstrate and clarify for students the procedure for asking another student for help. This should include examples and nonexamples of the appropriate voice tone, out of seat procedures, and the words to be used when asking another student for help.

3.3   The Fooler Game

Begin by gaining the student's attention. Then say, "We're going to play The Fooler Game." This means that the teacher will read the instructions for the independent work activity and then will ask (group and or individual) questions about the instructions to see if anyone can be fooled. If the students give a correct response, the teacher awards a point under the **YOU** side of the Fooler Chart (see illustration) and says something like, "Oh, I can't fool you! You were listening and paying attention to the instructions!" If the students give an incorrect response, the teacher awards a point on the **ME** side of the Fooler Chart, and says something like, "I fooled you!" If the students make an error the teacher should reread the appropriate part of the instructions that answers the question and then repeat the question to elicit a correct response.

FOOLER CHART	
YOU	**ME**
///	//

3.4 Emphasize Instructions

The teacher begins by telling the students that the instructions will be read aloud for their independent work assignment and then, he or she asks them questions about these instructions. The teacher should emphasize important words in the instructions when reading aloud. A signal is used to elicit group responses after each question is asked.

EXAMPLES

Instructions could include:

- "Listen to these instructions: Find the area of each rectangle."
- "Write the multiplication problem and the answer with the unit name. Now, get ready to answer questions about the instructions."

Questions could include:

- "What is the problem asking you to do?" (Find the area of each rectangle.)
- "What is the first step you will make?" (Write the multiplication problem.)
- "What is the next step you will make?" (Write the answer with the unit name.)
- "Does the problem tell you to find the area or the perimeter?" (To find the area.)
- "Will you write the answer, or the problem and the answer?" (The problem and the answer.)
- "What kind of name needs to be on the answer?" (The unit name.)
- "Think of one example of a unit name and tell your partner." (Examples could be miles, inches, feet.)

3.5 Highlight Key Words

Teach students the definition of key words and how to identify them in written material. Key words are words that stand out because they are bold faced, underlined, italicized, bulleted, etc. Key words are also verbs that tell you what to do. In the following sets of instructions, the key words have been underlined:

1. <u>Write</u> the <u>fractions</u> on each <u>number line</u>.

2. <u>Read</u> each statement <u>aloud</u>. <u>Decide</u> if the statement is <u>true</u> or <u>false</u>. Then <u>mark</u> a <u>±</u> <u>in front of</u> each <u>true statement</u>.

Provide the students with highlighter pens. The teacher should begin by reading aloud short instructions for an independent assignment. Then the teacher should identify the key words for the students and explain why the words identified are key. Next, tell them to highlight the key words in the same set of instructions that were just read aloud. Provide a lot of opportunities for guided practice with the key word concept. In addition, have students read and highlight the key words for each independent assignment before beginning the assignment. Check for understanding by monitoring which words have been highlighted and asking the student to explain the instructions.

3.6 Key Words Mean

Teach the students to recognize and define a variety of key words that frequently appear in assignments and tests. The vocabulary word and its definition can be put on the front and back side of flashcards. They can then be used for independent or partner practice, or referred to when completing work. The words that make up the definitions should be words that the students already know. Once students are proficient in identifying and defining the words, they can highlight or mark them as a first step in completing independent work assignments. The following are examples of defining key words in a level of language most students will comprehend.

(front)	(back)
apply	Ways in which the information can be used in a particular situation.
cause and effect	Define the events, tell the order, and why and how they happened.
classify	Tell how things or topics are alike.
compare	Show how characteristics of a concept are the same and different.
contrast	Show how characteristics of a concept are the same and different; stress the differences.
criticize	Explain how something was good or poor and how it could be made better.

I3: What can I do about the students who do not understand the independent assignment?

define	Tell how a word is like the group to which it belongs and then tell how it differs from others in the group.
diagram	Create a drawing, map, chart, or illustration.
discuss	Give an in depth explanation of the topic with a lot of examples.
evaluate	Identify the most important ideas, tell why they are important, give facts to support your answer.
explain	Give reasons or causes, discuss the order, point out problems, give details and examples to support your answer.
illustrate	Use examples or provide a diagram or picture proving your point.
interpret	Explain and give your own opinions about something.
justify	Give reasons for your answer.
list	Putting the words or answers in a series with numbers.
outline	Discuss major topics and show how they are related; identify details and show how they are related.
prove	Give facts to support your answer or argument.
relate	Show the connections between different ideas.
review	Give a summary and comment about the subject.
summarize	Point out the major ideas and tell how they are related.
trace	Tell about the development or progress of a concept or event.

I3: What can I do about the students who do not understand the independent assignment?

3.7   Getting the Help I Need

Teach students a strategy to use for getting assistance when they are unclear about an assignment or instructions. Either Ask for Help (G1.18) or Clarification (T12.8) can assist students in successfully getting the help they need.

3.8   Map the Instructions

Provide the students with a blank graphic organizer (see illustration) or teach them how to design their own for mapping out the steps required when completing longer independent assignments. Include a section to list points to keep in mind when completing the steps for each topic. There can be as many steps as necessary for each topic according to each student's needs.

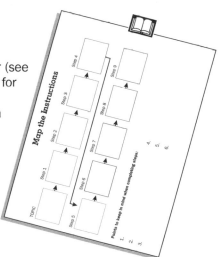

3.9   Instruction Cards (What, How, When/Where, Why)

Instruction cards are useful for students because the assignment is broken down into four basic elements: what, how, when/where, and why. The reasons and benefits of the assignment are clarified for students. Have them complete a card for each independent assignment by filling in the relevant information for each category.

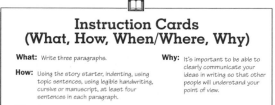

I3: What can I do about the students who do not understand the independent assignment?

3.10 Group Roles

 Assign each student in cooperative learning groups a role card. The role cards (see illustration) can be duplicated (one page per group of four) and cut up. Each student takes a role card for the independent work assignment. The responsibilities for each role need to be clearly defined and modeled for the students and should be clearly defined on the back of the role card. Have students switch cards and roles each new day.

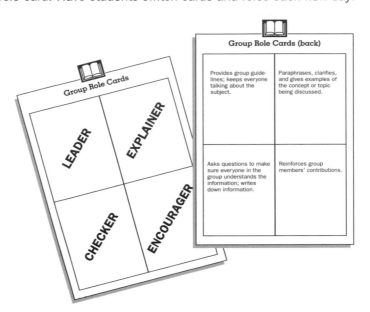

3.11 Independent Work Buddies

 Arrange students in dyads for completing independent work assignments. Provide dyads with one Work Buddies Scorecard (see illustration). The teacher awards dyads points for productive and attentive work that can be totaled each day and publicly posted. The scorecards can be disposed/recycled after one day or, if they are laminated, wiped off for reuse. Students can remain in their same dyads for one or more days.

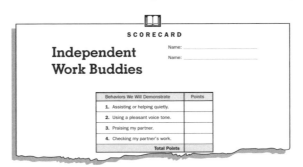

I3: What can I do about the students who do not understand the independent assignment?

4.1   Checking Station

Provide an area in the classroom where students can go to have their work checked by another student before turning it in. Stock the checking station with answer keys or tape recordings of correct answers for the student checker to use. If a paper to be turned in does not pass a predetermined criteria, students must make the necessary adjustments before it is handed in to the teacher.

4.2   Write the Steps

Have students write the steps involved with finding the answer instead of actually solving the problem.

EXAMPLES

- Problem:

$$\begin{array}{r} 14 \\ + \ 29 \\ \hline \end{array}$$

  The student writes:

  1. Add the ones column: 9 + 4.

  2. Write down the 3 and carry the 1.

  3. Add the tens column: 1 + 2 and the 1 that was carried.

- Instead of answering a question from a book, the student writes the steps to finding the answer.

  1. Read the question and identify the key words.

  2. Turn to page 15 where it talks about the main idea.

  3. Scan the page and locate the key words.

  4. Read the sentences that fall before and after the key words.

  5. Formulate an answer.

4.3   Checking and Completing

 Describe and model the steps for completing work and checking accuracy. The following steps can be used to improve students' overall performance and follow through.

Step 1: Focus on the task.

Step 2: Read all directions and circle key words.

Step 3: Explain to yourself what you need to do, and do it all.

Step 4: Ask for help if necessary.

Step 5: Check for completeness and correctness when proofing your work (see Proofing Skills, 14.4).

Step 6: Turn your assignment in.

4.4   Proofing Skills

 Describe and model examples of what proofing entails for different assignments. A student would utilize their proofing skills when checking for errors in a completed assignment or when returning to a previous assignment to correct mistakes made. Provide many practice opportunities for students and use visual charts of the steps as reminders. If the student is not familiar with a particular step in a proofing strategy, instruction on that step must take place prior to teaching the entire strategy.

EXAMPLES

The following proofing strategy can be used for math problems.

- Reread the problem.

- Reexamine the question.

- Check selection of operation.

- Recalculate and compare answers.

Source: Gable & Evans, 1993.

The following proofing strategy can be used when answering comprehension questions.

- Reread the question and circle the words that tell you how to answer the question, such as: list, define, compare, or explain. Next, underline what the question is talking about (i.e., the main idea) (e.g., rocks, presidents, story characters, etc).

- Check your answer to see how well it was done and if the main idea has been included.

For writing assignments, students can use the following mnemonic (COPS) for proofing.

- **C**apitalization
  Overall appearance
  Punctuation
  Spelling

Source: Schumaker et al., 1985.

Teach students editing symbols along with the proofing strategy so they can revise their own work.

⬭	Circle words spelled incorrectly.
/	Change a capital to a small letter.
≡	Change a small to capital letter.
∨	Add letters, words, or sentences.
⨀	Add a period.
⌐	Take out letters, words, or punctuation.
∧	Add a comma.
?	Anything you are unclear about.

These strategies work well in partner situations where students can proof one another's work after they have proofed their own.

4.5 Count Corrects and Errors

After completing an assignment, have students check their work and put a ✓ over the errors made and a **+** over the correct responses. Count up the total number of responses possible, the number of corrects, and the number of errors (see sample). Have students set an error limit for their assignment.

Worksheet

1. 28
   x 15
   140
   28
   420

2. 10
   x 10
   100

3. 9
   x 8
   72

4. 19
   x 20
   00
   38
   38

Name: _Margaret S._

Date	Total Possible	Corrects	Errors	Error Limit
5/2	19	15	4	29%

4.6 Accuracy Aims

Set aims ahead of time for the number of problems to be completed accurately. If students complete that number without error, provide reinforcement and up the aim by one. Have students keep track of progress made by using a tracker card or chart.

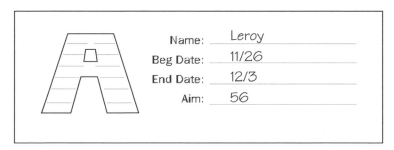

Name: _Leroy_
Beg Date: _11/26_
End Date: _12/3_
Aim: _56_

I4: What do I do about the students who do not check work for accuracy and completeness?

4.7   Challenge the Time

Determine the number of problems to be completed by students based on previous work. Set a timer for a specified amount of time and challenge each student to complete the work within that time frame. When appropriate, increase the number of problems to be completed, but keep the time frame constant. Have students keep track of performance and reinforce accordingly.

4.8   Check-Off List

Develop a self-monitoring checklist for students to use as they complete assignments or in-class work. For example, if a student is making errors because they are rushing or not following the correct procedures, identify the steps the student needs to follow. Write each step in order and then have the student check off each step on the list as it is completed. As the student becomes more aware of their accuracy, have him or her check the steps after completing two or three problems instead of every one. If necessary, combine this technique with a reinforcement for accuracy and completeness.

STEP	PROBLEM NUMBER									
	1	2	3	4	5	6	7	8	9	10
1. I copied the problem correctly.	✔	✔								
2. I divided the small number into the larger number.	✔	✔								
3. I multiplied the two numbers.	✔	✔								
4. I subtracted the correct numbers.	✔	✔								
5. I brought down the next number.	✔									
6. I started the process over.	✔									

4.9   Partners Plus

During independent work time, set a timer to sound at predetermined intervals. When the timer goes off, the students switch papers with their partners and correct the work completed. A plus (+) is awarded for every correct answer. The partners total the number of +s they have earned for that interval and record it on their Partner Scorecard. At the end of the activity, the total number of +s earned is tallied. Partners are awarded bonus points for their assignment by trading in +s earned. Bonus points can be added to assignment or quiz scores.

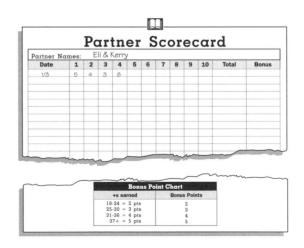

Partner Scorecard

Partner Names: Eli & Kerry

Date	1	2	3	4	5	6	7	8	9	10	Total	Bonus
1/3	5	4	3	8								

Bonus Point Chart

+s earned	Bonus Points
19-24 = 2 pts	2
25-30 = 3 pts	3
31-36 = 4 pts	4
37+ = 5 pts	5

I4: What do I do about the students who do not check work for accuracy and completeness?

5.1   Test Study Sheet

Study sheets for tests can be developed ahead of time and used throughout the lesson for students to review critical information they will need to know for the test. Study sheets provide students with the information regarding what to concentrate on, how to interpret questions, and the mechanics of test taking.

What to include on the study sheet:

1. Date of test.

2. Chapters to be covered.

3. Lecture outlines/notes that will be covered.

4. Other materials (films, videos, guest speakers).

5. Key vocabulary words.

6. Type of questions (true/false, multiple choice, short answer, essay).

7. Number of questions and point value.

8. Other information that may be helpful.

Chapter: *6*	Test Date: *2/14*

Test Study Sheet

What will be covered?   Insects

Lecture:
   2/1: Arthropods
   2/3: Arachnids

Notes:
   All

5.2   TERM

Model each of the steps listed for the TERM strategy. Help to illustrate the concept by using a variety of examples. Provide students with practice opportunities both in class and out of class to aid in generalization. Award points when students use the TERM studying strategy.

T—Take materials home (notes, books, assignments).
E—Examine and highlight what you know.
  Q—Question what you do not know.
  U—Underline what you think might be on the test.
  E—Emphasize and mark what you already know.
  S—Skim all reading material.
  T—Time schedule for studying.
  I —Invent test questions.
  O—Organize yourself.
  N—Never give up!
R—Review known material (anticipate possible questions).
M—Memorize new material (this is where to spend the bulk of your time).

Source: Frost, 1987.

5.3   Study Scheduling

Provide students with a copy of a weekly schedule broken into hour or half hour blocks of time. Students complete the schedule by writing in their weekly activities as well as their study schedule. Share with students the following suggestions for setting up a study schedule.

1. Plan regular study times.

2. Plan at least a half hour (younger students) or hour (older students) block of time in which to study.

3. Plan which assignments you are going to work on during the study time.

4. Take the first five minutes of each study activity to review what you have already learned and to plan what you are going to accomplish today. This helps promote long-term learning and a sense of accomplishment.

5. Plan breaks when studying for longer than one hour and stick to the allotted time.

6. Use daytime or early evening for study if possible. Most people are less efficient at night.

7. Work on the most difficult subjects when you are most alert.

8. Distribute your studying for a test over time rather than cram at the last minute.

9. Balance your activities between studying and other things. Allow time for recreational activities.

10. Reward yourself by crossing off items you complete on your schedule each time you meet a commitment.

Source: Bos & Vaughn, 1988.

I5: What can I do about the students who do not know how to prepare and/or study for a test?

5.4   Review Guides

The teacher can prepare a guide beforehand or the students can prepare one as they review for a test. Information that will assist students in preparing for an exam should be included.

EXAMPLES

- **Elementary**

  1. Topic: Story Problems.

  2. Terms: All together, remaining.

  3. Definitions: All together—add the numbers remaining; subtract the smaller number from the larger.

  4. Examples: (1) Tom had three balls, Joe had two. How many were there all together? (2) Mary had nine cookies, she ate two; how many cookies were remaining?

- **Secondary**

  1. Title/Subject: Rocks and Minerals.

  2. Purpose: Describe differences between rocks and minerals.

  3. Key vocabulary and definitions: igneous, metamorphic, sedimentary.

  4. Brief outline:

  5. Questions: What are three types of rocks?

  6. Text references: Pages 451-470.

5.5   Study Checklists

Distribute a checklist to students that includes important information about studying for an upcoming test. Teach and review the steps with students. Encourage students to share the checklist with parents and request assistance in using it while studying for a test. Points can be awarded to students for using the study checklist prior to a test.

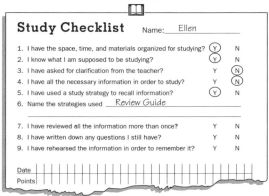

I5: What can I do about the students who do not know how to prepare and/or study for a test?

5.6   **Active Reading**

Teach students that when they need to memorize or study something carefully, they can use the following **RCRC** strategy.

Read: Read a little bit of material. Read it more than once. (For older students, read a paragraph and think about the topic and important details.)

Cover: Cover the material/paragraph with your hand.

Recite: Tell yourself what you have read. (For older students, state the topic and details in your own words.)

Check: Lift your hand from the material and check your answers.

If you forget something important, begin active reading again.

Source: Archer & Gleason, 1991.

5.7   **PREPARE**

Teach students the following strategy for test preparation. Provide explicit instruction and ample practice opportunities prior to administering a test.

Plan your time. Give yourself plenty of time to prepare. Do not cram the night before, instead take materials home daily.

Review notes to evaluate and code them according to what will be on the test.

Examine and highlight what you already know.

Practice definitions and lists with mnemonics or active reading.

Ask and Answer. Invent questions you think the teacher might ask and answer them.

Recite and memorize new material.

Expect to achieve. Positive self-talk will work wonders in helping you relax and feel confident.

5.8   **Write About**

Have students spend five minutes after a lesson writing about what took place during the lesson and what important information was learned. This can be written in a daily log or in the students' notebooks. The following questions can be used as prompts for this exercise.

1. What were the key concepts covered?

2. Develop a mnemonic for one piece of information.

3. Pick one concept and explain it in your own words.

4. Draw a graphic organizer relating the concepts of the chapter.

5. Choose three vocabulary words, identify the key words, and create practice cards.

I5: What can I do about the students who do not know how to prepare and/or study for a test?

After students have written their information individually, time can be spent sharing the information in groups or with partners. Allow time prior to the test to review what each student included in their Write About.

5.9   Information Coding

Teach students a method for coding notes, worksheets, and handouts that will assist them in recalling information for tests. Highlighter pens and/or symbols can be used for the coding. Provide students with suggestions for the codes or let them generate their own.

EXAMPLES

- Key concept   *
- Vocabulary word   ✓
- Need more information   ?
- Will be on test   +++
- Dates to remember   #
- Possible essay   E

After students have completed a daily lesson, give them a few minutes to review and code their notes, handouts, etc. This can be done individually or with a partner.

5.10   Map it Out

After the providing students with information on a topic, have them map it out (see illustration) for review as a class or individually. The maps can be kept in a folder to use when preparing for a test. The following mapping steps can be demonstrated to the class.

Step 1:   Find the topic.

Step 2:   Identify the key concepts related to the topic (subtopics).

Step 3:   Determine the supporting details for each key concept.

Step 4:   Use the map to recall the important information from the lesson.

Step 5:   Combine lesson maps to connect related topics covered in the entire unit.

I5: What can I do about the students who do not know how to prepare and/or study for a test?

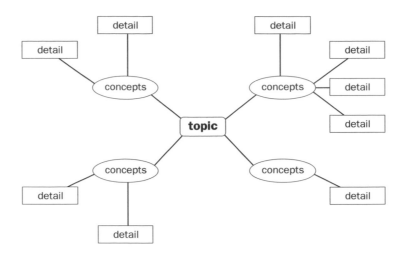

5.11 Practice Sheets

Teach students how to develop vocabulary practice sheets to review key vocabulary and concepts related to the unit of instruction. After each new concept is introduced, have students write the information on a split sheet of paper or an index card. Fold the sheet down the middle so the vocabulary words are on one side and the definitions on the other. Students can quiz themselves or work with partners. Use the practice sheets for review on a daily basis as well as at the end of the unit.

Entering the World of Work Chapter 2—Finding Jobs	
See/Say Facts	
1. Listings of businesses in the phone book.	1. Yellow Pages
2. A person or company that hires workers.	2. Employer
3. Shortened Words.	3. Abbreviations
4. Money a person receives after they no longer work.	4. Social Security
5. An office that matches workers with jobs.	5. Employment Agency
6. A meeting between an employer and a job applicant.	6. Interview
7. Working 40 or more hours per week.	7. Full-Time Job
8. Working less than 40 hours per week.	8. Part-Time Job
9. Shortened Words.	9. Abbreviations
10. A meeting between an employer and a job applicant.	10. Interview
11. Working 40 or more hours per week.	11. Full-Time Job

I5: What can I do about the students who do not know how to prepare and/or study for a test?

12.	Money a person receives after they no longer work.	12.	Social Security
13.	An office that matches workers with jobs.	13.	Employment Agency
14.	Working less than 40 hours per week.	14.	Part-Time Job
15.	Listings of businesses in the phone book.	15.	Yellow Pages
16.	A person or company that hires workers.	16.	Employer
17.	A meeting between an employer and a job applicant.	17.	Interview
(Fold along the middle line)			

Source: Lovitt et al., 1992.

I5: What can I do about the students who do not know how to prepare and/or study for a test?

Final Measurement

1.1   Testing Tips

The following are ideas to consider when it is necessary to make changes for students who require testing adaptations.

1. Shorten the length of the test.

2. Mark the minimal competency (see T1.7) items on the test and instruct students to only answer those items.

3. Define words and symbols such as difficult vocabulary or math symbols.

4. Circle or mark with a highlighter pen the key words that appear in the test instructions and in the test items.

5. Organize the test items from easy to more difficult.

6. Use simple sentences and a readability level that matches each student's reading level.

7. Make sure the items test what was taught.

8. Make sure that the responses to the test items reflect students' skills or knowledge, rather than their ability to write, read, spell, follow complicated instructions, etc.

9. Organize the test into sections and put boxes around those sections.

10. Administer the test in smaller sections rather than giving the entire test at one time.

11. Put test items in a computer-generated or printed format (clear, large font) which is familiar to the student and can be easily read.

12. Eliminate or replace difficult test question formats (i.e., essay) with an easier format (i.e., fill in the blank) that assesses the same knowledge.

13. Try timed tests or untimed tests depending on each student's preference.

14. Allow open book, open study guide, or open notes tests.

15. Only test students on the critical vocabulary and definitions.

16. Give students the outcomes and allow them to design/write the test.

F1: What can I do about the students who do not perform well with traditional test formats?

17. Administer the test orally and/or allow students to take the test orally.

18. Provide the students with options for test formats and ask them for their preference.

1.2   70/30 Splits

Design the unit performance assessments so that the individual test items represent minimal competency, advanced competency, and review competency information according to the following proportions:

1. **70%** of the items represent minimal competency information.

    Minimal competency information is the **must know** vocabulary, skills, concepts, etc. from the current unit that have been actively taught through teacher-directed instruction which all students are required to demonstrate.

2. **30%** of the items are split so that 15% represent **advanced competency** information and 15% represent **review competency** information.

    Advanced competency information is information that has not been directly taught through teacher-directed instruction, but rather information acquired through extension activities, exploration activities, independent study activities, etc. **Review competency** information is a sampling of minimal competency items from all previous end of unit performance assessments.

This type of arrangement allows certain students the opportunity to be successful on minimal competency information from the current unit and previous units, and achieve a passing grade on the test without being accountable for advanced competency information. In addition, more sophisticated students still have the opportunity to perform on advanced competency items.

Source: Sprick, 1985.

Introduction to Using Probes

The following seven examples describe quick ways for measuring student progress. Each activity involves the use of your own classroom curriculum. After spending some time each day teaching skills to students, you can use one of the following ideas for quickly measuring their progress.

These quick progress measures are called probes. Probes are somewhat like an end of unit assessment, but are less time consuming. Probes, unlike unit assessments, are given as often as possible (daily or several times a week) during the unit (instead of just at the end of the unit). It is not a problem for students to see a sampling of information from the entire unit on the probe. This focuses their attention on what is going to be coming up throughout the unit. Actually, students who use these probes repeatedly, do better than students who are just given an end of unit assessment. Probes are manageable because they are usually given for only one or two minutes each day.

Track students' scores on a chart so they can judge their performance frequently; it is almost like a daily report card. If things are not going too well, changes can be made immediately instead of waiting for six or eight weeks. Plus, the daily feedback that students receive on their progress is extremely motivating.

F1: What can I do about the students who do not perform well with traditional test formats?

When students attain the mastery level for a probe, the teacher can:

1. Give a more traditional unit assessment.

2. Move on to the next unit probe.

3. Involve the student in extension activities until the rest of the class passes the probe.

4. Have the student take review timings on probes that were already passed.

Probes are fun and should not create anxiety for students. They are like taking quick snapshots of student performance each day to see if learning is occurring. It is important to create a relaxed measurement environment by carefully introducing the idea of probes to students. Consider the following script as a way to introduce probes to the classroom.

> "Each day you will have an opportunity to take a picture of yourself during math. It is called a math probe. Instead of giving you a checkout at the end of the unit, I am going to give you the end of unit checkout every day. You should not be able to answer (write, say) any of the problems today because I haven't taught you these things yet. Each day I will teach you and then you will be able to answer more problems the next time we have our math probe. It will also be a check of my teaching. If you are not answering more questions each time we have our math probe, then it tells me I need to change something in my teaching. At the end of the unit (six to eight weeks from now) you will ace the math probe! That means you will know all of the answers. Now we will practice what I am talking about."

Teachers should answer these questions when creating any probe:

- What should I measure?

- How long do I measure?

- What materials do I need?

- How do I administer the probe?

- What should I expect students to be able to do?

1.3 Word Probes

What should I measure? Reading individual words (30 or more words) aloud which have been selected from a list of unknown words from a reading unit, book, or novel. These words should represent vocabulary that will appear in the unit of instruction.

How long do I measure? One minute.

What materials do I need? Two copies of the word list (one for the student and one for the recorder), one transparency to be placed over the recorder's (teacher's) copy so the word list can be reused, transparency pen, and accurate timer, preferably with an auditory signal.

How do I administer the probe?

1. Administer individually.

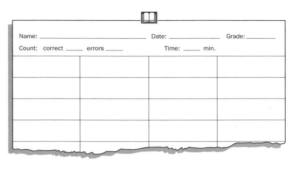

2. Say, "Please read these words aloud to me starting here. When you say the first word I will start the timer and listen to you read for one minute." (Demonstrate if necessary using a separate word list.) "Try to say each word. If you get stuck on a word for too long, I will tell you the word. You can skip words you do not know. Ready? Please begin."

3. Have the student read for one minute.

4. Put the word list under the transparency and place a slash on the copy to indicate where the student started reading.

5. As the student reads, place a mark (x) over any errors (mispronunciations, words skipped, and words given). If the student hesitates for two or three seconds, provide the word. Do not count an error if the student inserts words, self-corrects, sounds out, or repeats words.

6. At the end of the minute, place a slash on your copy to indicate the last word read by the student during the timing. Allow the student to finish reading the words rather than stopping after one minute.

7. Count the total number of words read correctly in one minute. Teach or assist the student to chart the correct and error information each time a probe is given. Discuss the student's current performance and expectations for future performance. Provide praise for daily improvements in the student's score.

What should I expect students to be able to do? By the end of the school year students should be able to say 60 to 80 correct words per minute with zero to one error per minute, on two separate occasions.

1.4   Oral Passage Probes

What should I measure? Reading aloud from a passage on the student's instructional level selected from a reader, textbook, library book, or functional reading materials such as newspapers and magazines. The passage should represent material that will be taught in class.

How long do I measure? One minute.

What materials do I need? Two copies of the passage (one for the student and one for the recorder with cumulative word counts at the end of each line, see illustration), one transparency to be placed over the recorder's (teacher's) copy so the passage can be reused, transparency pen, and accurate timer, preferably with an auditory signal.

How do I administer the probe?

1. Administer individually.

2. Say, "Please read this passage out loud to me starting here. When you say the first word I will start the timer and listen to you read for one minute." (Demonstrate if

necessary using a separate passage). "Try to say each word. If you get stuck on a word for too long I will tell you the word. You can skip words you do not know. Ready? Please begin."

3. Have the student read for one minute.

4. With the passage under the transparency, place a slash on the copy to indicate where the student started reading.

5. As the student reads, place a mark (x) over any errors (mispronunciations, words skipped, and words given). If the student hesitates for two to three seconds provide the word (see illustration below). Do not count an error if the student inserts words, self-corrects, sounds out, or repeats words.

6. At the end of the minute, place a slash on the copy to indicate the last word read by the student in one minute. Allow the student to finish reading the passage rather than stopping after one minute.

7. Count the total number of words read correctly and incorrectly in one minute. Teach or assist the student to chart the correct and error information each time the oral reading probe is given. Discuss the student's current performance and expectations for future performance. Provide praise for daily improvements in the student's score.

What should I expect students to be able to do? By the end of grade three, students should be able to read 150 to 250 correct words per minute with five or less errors per minute, on two separate occasions. (See chart on page 151 for additional grade levels and performance standards.)

Name ___Heather___ Date _____ Grade __1__

Count: correct __35__ error __5__ Time:_____ min.

The See-Saw

Jane was going to the store. She went down the street. She	(12)
saw a boy and a little dog.	(19)
The boy said, "Come and play with me. You may play with my	(32)
dog."	(33)
Jane said, "I will play with you. What can the dog do? He	(46)
is not very big."	(50)
"He is a good dog," said the boy. "He can run and jump. And	(64)
he can ride a see-saw."	(70)
"Oh, I want to see him ride," said Jane. "Where is it?"	(82)
"I have it in here," the boy said.	(90)
He said to the dog, "Go find the see-saw. We will have a	(104)
ride."	(105)

F1: What can I do about the students who do not perform well with traditional test formats?

The dog ran to the see-saw.	(112)
"Do you like to ride?" said the boy. "What do you say?"	(124)
The dog said, "Bow-wow!"	(129)
"Look at this," said the boy. "I am up and he is down.	(142)
Now he is up and I am down."	(150)
"What a funny ride for a dog!" said Jane.	(159)

1.5   Comprehension Probes

What should I measure? Information summarized in the student's own words based on free recall, pictures, listening, and silent or oral reading.

How long do I measure? One minute.

What materials do I need? Comprehension record sheet (see illustration), pencil, and accurate timer, preferably with an auditory signal.

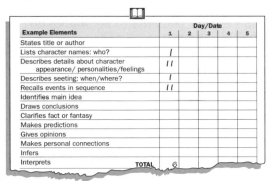

Example Elements	Day/Date				
	1	2	3	4	5
States title or author					
Lists character names: who?	I				
Describes details about character appearance/ personalities/feelings	I I				
Describes seeting: when/where?	I				
Recalls events in sequence	I I				
Identifies main idea					
Draws conclusions					
Clarifies fact or fantasy					
Makes predictions					
Gives opinions					
Makes personal connections					
Infers					
Interprets TOTAL	6				

How do I administer the probe?

1. Administer individually.

2. Say to the student, "When I say 'please begin,' tell me about the (experience, picture, story you listened to, material you read)." It may be necessary to demonstrate the summarizing procedure. "Keep telling me about the (insert topic) until I ask you to stop. I will keep track of what you tell me on this record sheet. Ready? Please Begin."

3. Provide prompts if the student stops summarizing before the minute elapses, such as: "Keep talking."; "Tell me more."; or "What else?"

4. Mark correct and error responses using a comprehension record sheet (see illustration).

5. Stop recording after one minute but allow the student to continue their thoughts.

6. Teach or assist the student to chart the correct and error information each time a comprehension probe is given. Discuss the student's current performance and

expectations for future performance. Provide praise for daily improvements in the student's score.

What should I expect students to be able to do? By the end of grade three students should be able to summarize 20 to 30 pieces of information per minute with two or less incorrect responses per minute, on two separate occasions.

> **Note:** Pieces of information include ideas and detail about ideas. For instance, the "purple dress" counts as two pieces of information. (See chart on page 151 for performance standards at different grade levels.)

1.6   Written Expression Probes

What should I measure? Words written in prose as a response to a story starter.

How long do I measure? One minute think time; three minutes writing time.

What materials do I need? Lined paper with story starter, pencils, transparency, transparency pen, overhead projector, and accurate timer, preferably with an auditory signal.

How do I administer the probe?

1. Administer individually or with entire group.

2. Say, "Today I want you to write a story on the lined paper. I will read the sentence to you at the top of the page, then you will write your story about what happens next." (Demonstrate the procedure for the students using the overhead transparency.)

3. Then say, "I will give you one minute to think about what you want to write and then I will give you three minutes to write. Please begin thinking."

4. After the thinking time has elapsed, "Please start writing."

5. After the three minutes, "Please stop. Put your pencils down. Thank you."

6. Teach or assist the student to count the number of words that were written. Correct words include intelligible words that make sense in the story. Words do not need to be spelled correctly unless included as part of the criteria for mastery.

7. Teach or assist the student to chart the total number of correct and error words. Discuss the student's current performance and expectations for future performance. Provide praise for daily improvements in the student's score.

What should I expect students to be able to do? Thirty to forty correct words per minute with two or less errors (e.g., punctuation, spelling, capitalization, verb agreement, etc.) per minute, on two separate occasions.

Name _____Erica_____   Date ____2/24____   Time____3 minutes____

Last weekend my friend and I went skiing and . . .

We were so excited to finally be cruising down the powdery, free slopes; there wasn't enough time in the world. As we were preparing to get off the lift and continue skiing, I felt a tugging at my pants. I didn't think much of it until I stood up to ski off. The suspenders of my outfit had caught onto the bars of the chair lift and before I knew it, I was hanging upside down. The unknowing chairlift operator kept going until it went all the way around. How embarrassing!

Correct Words   =   89
Incorrect   =   3

F1: What can I do about the students who do not perform well with traditional test formats?

1.7   **Math Probes**

What should I measure? Digits written when computing math problems.

How long do I measure? One minute.

What materials do I need? Response sheet, pencils, answer key, transparency demonstration sheet, transparency pen, overhead projector, and accurate timing device, preferably with an auditory signal.

How do I administer the probe?

1. Administer to an individual student or the entire group.

2. Say, "When I say, 'Please begin,' you will write the answers to these math problems as quickly and carefully as you can." The response sheet can be put in a folder under an acetate sheet taped inside the folder. Students can use a transparency pen to write their answers. Using this procedure, the response sheet does not need to be duplicated each time a new student takes the probe. This procedure can also be demonstrated using an overhead transparency.

3. If the response sheet includes problems with different operation signs, point this out to the students. For students with less skills, the response sheet can include only one type of problem, or have them simply write numbers.

4. Next, "If you have trouble with a problem, try it, write something, and then move on to the next problem. Do not erase. Ready? Please begin."

5. After one minute has elapsed, "Please stop. Put your pencils down. Thank you."

6. Provide answer keys for correction and counting. (If using acetate sheets, the answer key can be duplicated on the back side of the response sheet and placed under the acetate for easy correction.) Teach or assist students to count the number of **correct digits** (not answers) written. For example: $7 + 6 = 13$ would be counted as two digits correct ('1' and '3'); $9 \times 4 = 35$ would be counted as one digit correct ('3') and one error ('5'). For more involved problems, points could be given for equal and operation signs, lines, numbers carried, proper alignment of numbers, or commas (see illustration).

$$
\begin{array}{r}
\overset{3}{}\overset{7}{} \\
\overset{2}{}\overset{5}{} \\
249 \\
\times\ \ 86 \\
\hline
1494 \\
1992 \\
\hline
21{,}414
\end{array}
$$

Count 20

(13 digits, 1 alignment, 4 digits carried, 1 line to separate answer, 1 comma)

$$
\begin{array}{r}
1\,{}^{1}/_{4} = 1\,{}^{3}/_{12} \\
+3\,{}^{2}/_{3} = 3\,{}^{8}/_{12} \\
\hline
4\,{}^{11}/_{12}
\end{array}
$$

Count 19

(2 equal signs, 13 digits, 3 fraction lines, and 1 line to separate answer)

7. Teach or assist the students to chart the total number of correct and error digits. Discuss each student's current performance and expectations for future performance. Provide praise for daily improvements in students' score.

What should I expect students to be able to do? By the end of grade three students should be able to figure seventy to ninety correct digits per minute with one or less errors per minute, on two separate occasions.

F1: What can I do about the students who do not perform well with traditional test formats?

1.8 Social Skill Probes

What should I measure? Demonstration of socially appropriate/inappropriate behavior in school, home, and community settings. For example: Following Instructions, Accepting Feedback, Making a Greeting, Making a Request, Getting the Teacher's Attention, Disagreeing Appropriately, Apologizing, Engaging in a Conversation, Giving a Compliment, etc.

How long do I measure? Variable depending on the social skill being measured.

What materials do I need? If self-recording: a tracker card, a counting device, a timing device.

How do I administer?

1. Determine the social skill to be observed. Whenever possible, teach the students to observe and record their own behavior.

2. Determine a setting for observation and recording, such as during role play, in the classroom, on the playground, at home, at a work setting.

3. Determine an appropriate length of time for observation. This should ideally be a standard time for each observation period. This could be 30 minutes for Getting the Teacher's Attention, one hour for Following Instructions, or an entire school day for Engaging in Conversations.

4. Define the behavioral components for the social skill so that it can be easily counted. (See the pocket tracker card illustration.) For example, **Engaging in a Conversation** could be defined as:

    (a) Look at the person; (b) Use a pleasant voice tone; (c) Ask the person questions; (d) No interruptions; (e) After the person's answer, make a comment without changing the subject.

5. Teach or assist students to count the number of occurrences of the behavior during the observation time. (See the behavior components illustration.) Teach or assist students to chart the number of occurrences of appropriate and inappropriate behavior. While referring to the chart, discuss each student's current performance and expectations for future performance. Provide praise for daily improvements in each student's performance.

F1: What can I do about the students who do not perform well with traditional test formats?

What should I expect students to be able to do? Students should display 99% or more appropriate social behaviors during socially engaged time in school, home, leisure, or work environments, on two separate occasions.

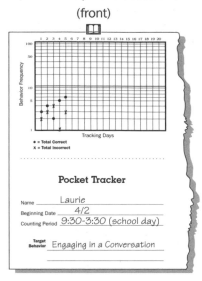

Source: Fister & Kemp, 1994.

1.9   Content Area/Functional Skill Probes

When teaching in the content areas (i.e. social studies, science, English literature, biology, current events, community awareness, health and safety, etc.) it is effective to individually measure a student's ability to:

1. **Communicate** (talk or write about the subject matter so as to be understood and understand others).

2. **Clarify Values or Opinions** (being able to provide a range of opinions related to the topic/issue).

3. **Problem Solve/Make Decisions/ Determine Consequences** (interpreting content area information to solve problems, make decisions, and predict results).

EXAMPLES

*   The measurement for a Science/Cell Biology objective where students will correctly use 18 of the 20 critical ("must know") vocabulary and 15 of the 17 critical ("must know") concepts in cell biology might be:

    1. A ten-minute written narrative summary.

    2. A two-minute paraphrasing summary.

    3. A one-minute oral summary.

- The measurement for a History/Economic Depressions objective where students will evaluate government programs for stimulating prosperity and compare and contrast unemployment problems of the 1930s and the 1990s might be:

  1. A ten-minute oral summary.

  2. A five-minute debate.

  3. A ten-minute written comparison.

- The measurement for a Drug and Alcohol objective where students will describe ideas for nurturing themselves might be:

  1. A one-minute written summary.

  2. A 30-second commercial.

  3. A 30-second recap of an illustrated magazine advertisement.

Source: Starlin, 1989.

Suggested Performance Standards
(Guidelines to Use With Probes)

PINPOINT	STANDARD
Reading	
See/Say Isolated Sounds	60-80 sounds/minute
See/Say Phonetic Words	60-80 words/minute
Think/Say Alphabet (forward or back)	400+ letters/minute
See/Say Letter Names	80-100 letters/minute
See/Say Sight Words	80-100 words/minute
See/Say Words in Context (oral reading)	200+ words/minute
See/Think Words in Context (silent reading)	400+ words/minute
Think/Say Ideas or Facts	15-30 ideas/minute
Handwriting	
Emphasizing Speed	
See/Write Slashes	200-400 slashes/minute
See/Write Circles	100-150 circles/minute
Think/Write Alphabet	80-100 letters/minute
Emphasizing Accuracy	
See/Write Letters (count three per letter)	75 correct/minute
See/Write Cursive Letters Connected (count three per letter)	125 correct/minute
Spelling	
Hear/Write Dictated Words	80-100 letters/minute
Hear/Write Dictated Words	15-25 words/minute
Math	
See/Write Numbers Random	100-120 digits/minute
Think/Write Numbers (zero through nine serial)	120-160 digits/minute
See/Say Numbers	80-100 numbers/minute
Think/Say Numbers in Sequence (count-by)	150-200+ numbers/minute
See/Write Math Facts	70-90 digits/minute

Source: Beck, 1976.

F1: What can I do about the students who do not perform well with traditional test formats?

2.1 Confidence Building

Post the following steps in the classroom and discuss how using this technique during a test will reduce anxiety and build confidence. Prior to a test, practice this procedure with the students so they will be comfortable using it on their own.

Step 1: Close your eyes before you begin the test.

Step 2: Take a deep breath and hold it for five seconds. Slowly blow out the air. Repeat three times.

Step 3: After the third breath, keep your eyes closed and remind yourself that you are well prepared for the exam.

Step 4: Imagine the teacher handing back your test with a good grade on it.

Source: Greene & Jones-Bamman, 1985.

2.2 Test-Taking Awareness

Instruct the students in the general techniques used to prepare for any test. Explain and demonstrate each of the following tips by providing students with examples and nonexamples.

1. Review the entire test.

2. Know the allotted time for the test.

3. Know the point value for each question.

4. Read and follow directions carefully.

5. Underline key words in directions.

6. Answer questions you are sure of first.

7. Mark the questions you need to come back to later.

8. Return to questions that are marked.

9. Review all questions to be sure they are completed.

F2: What can I do about the students who do not use strategies for taking a test?

2.3   Knowing the Question

Teach the student specific methods for answering a wide range of test questions.

EXAMPLES

True/False Items

- To be true, everything in the question must be true; only one detail needs to be false for the answer to be false.

- Be sure qualifiers are understood. Words such as always, none, only, and all are likely to be found in false statements. Words such as usually, generally, sometimes and certain, tend to make statements true.

- Simplify questions by crossing out double negatives and then answer the question.

- First impressions are usually correct.

Multiple Choice Items

- Determine how the question is to be answered (circle the response or write the number next to the question).

- Use the process of elimination: cross out the answers you know are wrong.

- Look for exact answers.

- The longest answer is often correct because more information is usually necessary to make a correct statement.

- Answers with qualifiers are often correct.

Matching Items

- Determine if there are an equal number of items in each column.

- Begin with the easiest items and individually focus on each and its match.

- Cross out items as they are matched to avoid confusion.

Short Answer/Completion Items

- Read the question carefully to determine what is being asked.

- Use cues such as the number of blank spaces.

- Be sure the answer is logical and grammatically correct.

Essay Questions

- Read the question carefully and identify key words to help determine how to set up your answer.

- Plan time for organizing, writing, and proofreading.

- Organize your answer by jotting down your ideas or outlining them using a web or map.

- Write on every other line to make changes easier.

- Respond to all the information in the question.

F2: What can I do about the students who do not use strategies for taking a test?

2.4   Posttest Checklist

After students have taken a test and it has been returned, have them respond to a list of questions related to successful test-taking procedures.

Have students determine what areas they need to concentrate on for the next test. Use the information on the checklist to conference with students and provide additional strategies for test taking.

Posttest Checklist

1. Did you put your name, date, and class period on the test?   (Y) N
2. Did you read all the instructions and preview the test before responding to questions?   (Y) N
3. Did you set up a time frame for completing the test?   Y (N)
4. Did you answer all questions?   Y (N)
   How many were correct? __45__   Incorrect? _5_
5. Did you check your work before turning it in?   (Y) N
6. What question types did you answer best? ___Essay___

7. What question types can you improve upon?_____
   _____Short answer_____

2.5   Math Problem Solving

Provide students with steps that will help them solve problems on math tests. Demonstrate each of the steps using a variety of math problems.

Step 1: Read the question carefully.

Step 2: Use key words to determine the following:
   a. What do you need to find out? (i.e., What is the question asking?)
   b. What operations will you use?
   c. How many steps are there?
   d. What is the order of the steps?

Step 3: Cross out information not needed and make a list of the necessary information in sequence.

Step 4: Use drawings to help visualize the problem.

Step 5: Write neatly and align numbers to avoid mistakes.

Step 6: Check your work carefully.

2.6   RIDGES

Teach students the following mnemonic to facilitate understanding and organization of mathematical word problems. Examples and nonexamples of each step should be demonstrated and practiced prior to using the strategy.

Read the problem. Be sure you understand what the problem is asking. Reread if necessary.

I know statements. List all the information in the problem.

Draw a picture. Include all the information from the "I Know" statements.

Goal statement. Write "I want to know." This assists students with clues for the next step.

Equation development. Write an equation to solve the problem.

Solve the equation. Plug in the necessary information to reach the goal and solve the problem.

_____
Source: Snyder, 1987.

F2: What can I do about the students who do not use strategies for taking a test?

2.7 PIRATES

Teach time-management techniques for test taking by providing examples and nonexamples of each of the steps in the PIRATES strategy.

Prepare to Succeed. Write PIRATES and your name on the top of test; determine the allotted time and order for each section; say something positive and start within two minutes.

Inspect the instructions. Read the instructions carefully, underline how and where to respond, notice special requirements.

Read, remember, reduce. Read the whole question, remember through strategies, and reduce choices.

Answer or abandon. Answer the question if you know it, abandon the question if you are not sure.

Turn Back. Turn back to abandoned questions when you are at the end of the test. Encourage yourself to earn extra points.

Estimate. **A**void absolutes; **C**hoose the longest or most detailed choice; **E**liminate identical choices.

Survey. Check to insure all questions are answered; change an answer only if you are absolutely sure.

Source: Hughes, Schumaker, Deshler, & Mercer, 1987.

3.1 Performance Tracking Sheets

Provide the student with a tracking sheet for the unit or chapter that outlines the class activities, assignments, and tests with their corresponding point value. Have the students keep the tracking sheet in their notebooks. Each time a grade is given, instruct students to immediately record the information on the sheet. This information will allow students to monitor their own performance throughout the unit.

Name: Jeremy	
Unit: Airplanes	
1. Worksheet	10 / 12
2. Worksheet	12 / 12
3. Worksheet	9 / 12
4. Notes	12 / 15
5. Chapter Questions	16 / 20
6. Vocabulary	17 / 10
7. Quiz	25 / 65
8. Quiz	24 / 25
9. Project	40 / 50
10. Test	98 / 100
Total Points	263/321

3.2 Performance Conference

Set up a five-minute meeting with each student in the class during independent work. These meetings should occur on a weekly basis in order to review the student's performance in the class. Information related to the students assignments, class participation, test scores, and/or behavior can be discussed at the conference. The student or teacher should keep anecdotal records on the outcome of the meetings that are included in a student's folder or portfolio. This technique can be combined with Performance Choices (F3.7), Checkouts (F3.3), or Tracking Sheets (F3.1).

3.3 Performance Checkouts

Have students keep records of their daily or weekly performance in class. A chart (see illustration) can be used to assist students in monitoring progress throughout the entire unit of instruction. At the end of the week, students check off each assignment or activity they have worked on during the week by placing a checkmark in the corresponding column. In the grade column (G) the student determines their own performance grade for the week in each area. A simple system such as **E** (Excellent), **S** (Satisfactory) and **N** (Needs Improvement) can be used. The teacher then reviews each student's sheet and writes feedback statements about their performance on each assignment. The students then write a goal for the next week based on both their own evaluation of the work done and the teacher's feedback. The sheet is initialed by both the teacher and the student and kept in a portfolio or notebook.

3.4   Performance Journal

Have students respond to questions related to their class performance by writing in a journal on a regular basis. This information can be included in students' portfolios or can be incorporated into the grading system. The following are some questions related to student performance which might be included in a performance journal.

EXAMPLES

- I think I am earning an/a _____ grade in this class because . . . .

- If I had to describe my performance in this class, I would say . . . .

- I would compare my performance in this class to . . . .

- Another classmate would describe me as a _____ worker because . . . .

- I am doing great, ok, or poorly in this class because . . . .

3.5   Charting

Use Probes described in F1.3-9, as a way to measure student performance on a frequent basis. Students can be taught how to keep track of their scores by recording them on a chart. Displaying the scores on a chart provides students with immediate feedback and a picture of their ongoing performance. After several scores (five through eight) have been recorded on the chart, each student, with assistance from the teacher, can make important decisions about their progress. The tracking chart should have the following features:

1. The extended curved line is drawn just before the day measurement begins. The specific objective is written along the curved line to show what is being measured (e.g., "Say Unit One Words").

2. A large capital 'A' (representing the aim or goal) is drawn on the chart. The bar of the 'A' crosses at the level at which the teacher expects the student to be performing (i.e., correct responses) after several weeks of instruction. An inverted 'A' can also be placed on the chart to show the level of incorrect responses at which the teacher expects the student to be performing after several weeks of instruction.

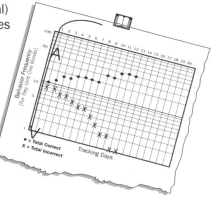

3. The student records their performance after each probe by marking their correct/appropriate score with a ● and their incorrect/inappropriate score with an **X**.

F3: What can I do about the students who do not monitor work performance?

4. When the student's ●s and **X**s reach the level for at least two consecutive days, another curved line can be drawn on the chart to show that measurement begins for a new objective.

> **Note:** Certain circumstances may warrant a decision to move onto another unit objective before the student has achieved their current aim.

Source: Beck, 1976.

3.6 Goal Setting

Assist students in setting performance goals for themselves that are beyond their present level of performance. Do this by letting them know how they are currently doing and explaining how to select a reasonable goal. Help students decide if they need to work on daily, weekly, or monthly goals. Then, have students write goals and action steps that will help them to achieve each goal. In addition, discuss how the students can be rewarded if the goal is met. Require students to complete periodic progress reports related to their goal by charting the information or keeping anecdotal reports.

Goal Setting

Goal Action Chart

What I Will Do:	How Long It Will Take:	Exp. Comp. Date:
Goal: Say 30 facts after reading	3 weeks	2/7

Steps: Create outlines.
Highlight key words.
Write down words/concepts I don't know.

Name: Isaac   Starting Date: 1/15
How I will reward myself: Trip to the bookstore with Dad

3.7 Performance Choices

At the beginning of every unit pass out a choice sheet similar to the one in the illustration. Have each student fill out the sheet and turn it in for teacher approval. Have students review the sheet throughout the unit to monitor the completion of activities and their performance. This sheet allows students to make choices about the work they will do and provides feedback on their progress throughout the unit.

Name __Latrice__   Date __5/16__

I will do five of the following to show I understand the material in Chapter _____.
(Everyone must complete the circled items.)

_____	1.	Design a filmstrip of the major points.
✔	2.	Write a summary of each of the major points and answer the questions at the end of the chapter.
_____	3.	Give a five minute oral report on _____.
✔	4.	Discuss the major points with two peers over a tape recorder.
✔	5.	Complete _4_ / _5_ worksheets.
✔	(6.)	Take the final test.
✔	(7.)	Complete a notebook of major facts.
_____	8.	Another option approved by the teacher.

F3: What can I do about the students who do not monitor work performance?

4.1 Combination Grading

Combination grading involves the use of different performance measures such as demonstrations, interviews, projects, portfolios, exhibits, oral tests, written tests, matching items, short answer items, etc. Each of the student's scores are averaged together to arrive at a letter grade, pass/incomplete, or credit/no credit grade.

4.2 Coded Grading

Coded grading utilizes three levels (A1, A2, A3, B1, B2, B3, etc.) within each of the standard letter grades. The numbers assigned to each letter grade could represent the following:

1 = based on use of **above** grade-level material or **advanced** competencies..

2 = based on use of **on** grade-level material or **minimal** competencies.

3 = based on use of **below** grade-level material or **adapted** competencies.

For instance, awarding a student with an A1 would indicate that the student earned a standard grade of A using material above the student's actual grade-level placement. A grade of C3 would indicate that the student earned a standard grade of C using material below the student's actual grade level.

Source: DeBoer, 1994.

F4: What can I do about the students who do not respond to traditional grading procedures?

4.3   Asterisk Grading

Letter grades are awarded to students and may include an asterisk. An asterisk indicates that certain accommodations were made in order to meet the needs of that student. The specific accommodations used for a particular student would be indicated by marking the appropriate items on a checklist (see illustration for example) that is attached to the report card.

Accommodation Checklist

✔	Test read to the student.
_____	Student dictated answers to teacher/another student.
_____	Tests explained in detail/reviewed prior to taking them.
_____	Materials audio taped for the student.
_____	Materials video taped for the student.
_____	Study guides/graphic organizers provided during lecture.
✔	Additional time provided for work/test completion.
_____	Instructional objectives prioritized and reduced.
_____	Instructional objectives adapted.

Source: Adapted from DeBoer, 1994.

4.4   A/B/C/Not Yet

A/B/C/Not Yet (or Incomplete) is based on a mastery learning premise that all students will succeed. If a student does not demonstrate minimal competency performance or above, then a **"Not Yet"** is given and reteaching is provided.

Source: DeBoer, 1994.

4.5   Double Grading

Double grading involves giving the student two grades such as A/C or C/C. The top grade represents the student's learning over the instructional time period, compared to their beginning performance. The bottom grade represents the students performance compared to the entire class' performance.

Source: DeBoer, 1994.

F4: What can I do about the students who do not respond to traditional grading procedures?

4.6   Challenge Grading

Challenge grading involves the assignment of differing point values on test questions (or other performance measures such as demonstrations, interviews, projects, portfolios, exhibits, etc.) based upon their difficulty level.

EXAMPLE

The student would have the option of answering:

- A group of ten easier level questions/tasks valued at ten points each (total 100).

- A group of five slightly more difficult questions/tasks valued at 20 points each (total 100).

- A group of four more difficult questions/tasks valued at 25 points each (total 100).

- Two even more difficult questions/tasks valued at 50 points each (total 100).

- One very difficult question/task valued at 100 points.

The difficulty level of questions can be varied by modifying the question type (i.e., true/false, multiple choice, fill in the blank, short answer, essay, projects, etc.) and/or the level of cognition that is expected (i.e., list, define, compare, contrast, develop, evaluate, critique, etc.).

Source: DeBoer, 1994.

4.7   IEP Grading

A student who qualifies and is eligible for special education services has an **Individualized Education Plan** (**IEP**) which has been developed by a team of professionals. The IEP may dictate requirements such as instructional procedures, evaluation procedures, grading procedures, and/or graduation requirements. In this case, procedures specified in the student's IEP must be adhered to and implemented by those who are responsible for delivering the educational services.

4.8   Contract Grading

Grade contracts are formal arrangements that are negotiated between individual students and the teacher. The students can be offered different options for demonstrating performance on the stated objectives or adapted objectives. Performance measures can include tests, demonstrations, interviews, projects, portfolios, exhibits, etc. An agreement should be reached that is acceptable to both the student and the teacher (see illustration). A grading contract should include the following components:

1. The type of work to be completed by the student.

2. The quantity and quality of work to be completed.

Grading Contract

I, _____Melinda_____, agree to the following objectives:

1. _Complete Reading Assignments_____

2. _____

3. _____

I agree to complete the following activities to demonstrate mastery of the above stated objectives:

1. _Start homework with plenty of time_____

2. _Review regularly_____

F4: What can I do about the students who do not respond to traditional grading procedures?

3. The signatures of the teacher, student, and parent (when appropriate).

4. Timelines for the completion of work.

F4: What can I do about the students who do not respond to traditional grading procedures?

Quick
Reference Guide

 # Quick Reference Guide

*Note: Reproducibles are available for reproduction in the companion book, *TGIF: Making It Work On Monday.*

TECHNIQUE	QUESTION	NUMBER	REPRODUCIBLE	PAGE #
A/B/C/Not Yet	F4	4		162
All Talk Together	T9	2		51
All Together	T12	5		64
Alternating Buddies	G1	4		70
Answer, Pair, Spotlight	T12	7		64
Ask, Pause, Call	T12	1		63
Ask Three Before Me	I3	2		121
Assignment Buddies	I1	1		109
Assignment Questions	G1	7		71
Asterisk Grading	F4	3		162
Beat the Clock	G1	6		71
Change the Channel	G3	1		81
Checking Station	I4	1		127
Coded Grading	F4	2		161
Cognitive Shift	T1	1		15
Color Coding	G2	1		77
Colored Pencils	G1	10		72
Combination Grading	F4	1		161
Condition Shift	T1	2		17
Confidence Building	F2	1		153
Consult	T12	4		64
Contribution Chips	G5	5		101
Contribution Points	G5	4		101
Cooperation Keys	G4	1		93
Cut-Up	G1	9		71
Daily Checkout	I2	1		115
Defend Your Position	T11	1		59
Double Grading	F4	5		162
Effective Praise	G1	1		69
Emphasize Instructions	I3	4		122
Everybody Say	T4	1		29
Five-Minute Reviews	T11	2		59

TECHNIQUE	QUESTION	NUMBER	REPRODUCIBLE	PAGE #
Fooler Game, The	I3	3		121
Formulate, Share, Listen, Create	T9	4		52
Frequent Questions	T4	2		29
Get Ready	T2	1		21
Group/Individual Questioning	T8	1		47
Highlighting	T5	1		33
Highlight Key Words	I3	5		123
Huddle	G5	1		101
I am Ready	T8	3		47
I am Working/I Need Help Sign	I3	1	*	121
I Can Say It	T2	4		21
Listen, Write, Listen, Say	G3	5		82
Listening Cues	T2	2		21
Name's Up Listening Board	T4	4		30
Name's Up Volunteer Board	T8	5		48
No Surprises	T12	6		64
On-Task Chart	T4	3	*	30
Oral Reading Points	G2	2	*	77
Page Numbers	G3	2		81
Participation Board	T3	1		25
Participation Buddies	T3	2		25
Partner Board	G4	2		93
Pass for Now	T12	3		63
Pens in the Jar	G5	6		102
Please Come Back	T8	4		48
Please Come Back	T9	7		52
Prequestioning	T9	6		52
Product Shift	T1	4		18
Proficiency Shift	T1	3		17
Prompts	T9	5		52
Question/Instruction Repeat	G3	4		82
Questions First	G3	3		81
Rapid-Fire Questions	T9	8		52
Rationale Questions	T6	1		37
Rationale Statements	G1	3		70
Recycling	T5	2		33
Responses Without Talking	T8	2		47

TECHNIQUE	QUESTION	NUMBER	REPRODUCIBLE	PAGE #
Restate	T12	2		63
Share Your Reasons	T6	3		37
Signals	G5	3		101
Star Stickers	G1	8		71
Step Out	G4	3		94
Stop/Go Folders	I2	2		115
Strategic Skills	G1	5		70
Think About That	T9	1		51
Think and Say Ideas	T9	9		53
Think and Say Why	T6	2		37
Think Out Loud	G1	2		69
Think Out Loud	I1	2		109
Think, Pair, Share	T9	3		51
Write and Speak	G5	2		101
Write the Steps	I4	2		127
You-Me Game	T2	3		21

 **Quick Reference Guide**

*Note: Reproducibles are available for reproduction in the companion book, *TGIF: Making It Work On Monday*.

TECHNIQUE	QUESTION	NUMBER	REPRODUCIBLE	PAGE #
70/30 Splits	F1	2		142
Accuracy Aims	I4	6		129
Active Reading	I5	6		134
Activity Change	T1	5		18
Add It Up	G3	11	*	85
Advance Organizers	T11	3		60
Am I Working?	I1	4		109
Answer Experts	G3	10	*	84
Ask for Help	G1	18	*	75
Assignment Aims	G1	16	*	74
Assignment Banking	I1	7	*	111
Assignment Champion Notebook	I2	11	*	119
Assignment Co-Op	G4	7		96
Assignment Contracts	I2	9	*	118
Assignment Initials	I1	6	*	110
Assignment Log	I1	9	*	111
Assignment Notebooks	I1	13		113
Attribute Maps	T7	11		46
Behavior Bingo	G1	14		73
Behavior Bingo	T2	7		23
Buddy Carbon Notes	T10	1		55
Buddy Nose (Knows)	T2	6	*	22
Cause/Effect	G3	14	*	86
Challenge Grading	F4	6		163
Challenge the Time	I4	7		130
Change the Channel	G1	12		72
Charting	F3	5	*	158
Check-Off List	I4	8		130
Checking and Completing	I4	3	*	128
Clarification	T12	8	*	64
Classwide Peer Tutoring	G4	9		98
Completion Dots	G1	17		74

TECHNIQUE	QUESTION	NUMBER	REPRODUCIBLE	PAGE #
Comprehension Outlines	G3	20	*	88
Comprehension Probes	F1	5	*	146
Comprehension Wheels	G3	17	*	87
Concept Angles	T7	4		43
Content Area/Functional Skill Probes	F1	9		150
Contract Grading	F4	8	*	163
Contribution Aims	G5	12	*	104
Cooperative Notes	T10	7	*	58
Corners	G5	7		102
Corrective Feedback	T7	3		42
Corrective Feedback	T9	11		53
Count Corrects and Errors	I4	5		129
Counting Responses	T12	10	*	65
Countoon	T4	9	*	32
Design Your Own	G1	15	*	73
Draw-a-Name	T12	9		65
Draw-a-Name	T8	8		49
Fill in the Dots	I2	10	*	119
Folded Corners	T8	7		49
Following Instructions	T2	5	*	22
Following Instructions	T4	5		30
Four-Fold	T10	2	*	55
Futures Map	T6	5	*	38
Getting the Help I Need	I3	7		125
Getting the Teacher's Attention	T4	7	*	31
Goal Setting	F3	6	*	159
Graffiti Papers	G5	8		102
Graphic Organizers (Partial)	T10	8		58
Graphic Organizers (Sequence)	T7	10		45
Graphic Organizers (Top Down)	T5	7		36
Graphic Organizers	G3	25		91
Group Roles	I3	10	*	126
Heads Together	T8	6		48
Herringbone	G3	16	*	86
Hit the Homework Target	I2	6	*	117
Home/School Folders	I2	4	*	116
Home/School Talk	I2	3	*	116

TECHNIQUE	QUESTION	NUMBER	REPRODUCIBLE	PAGE #
Homework Teams	I2	7		117
Homework Tracking Charts	I2	5	*	116
How Do I Rate?	I2	12	*	119
I am Ready to Find Out	G3	7	*	83
I Question That!	T7	6		43
IEP Grading	F4	7		163
Independent Work Buddies	I3	11	*	126
Index Cards	T10	3		56
Information Coding	I5	9		135
Inside/Outside Circle	G5	9		103
Instruction Cards (What, How, When/Where, Why)	I3	9	*	125
Keeping the Numbers Low	T4	6		31
Key Words	G3	6		83
Key Words Mean	I3	6	*	123
Know/Do Not Know	G3	19	*	87
Know/Want to Know/Learned (KWL)	T7	7		44
Knowing the Question	F2	3		154
Learning Logs	T7	8	*	44
LITES	T10	5	*	56
Magic Pens	G2	5		79
Make the GRADE	I1	5	*	110
Making a Contribution	G5	10	*	103
Map it Out	I5	10		135
Map the Instructions	I3	8	*	125
Mark and Say Main Idea	G3	9		84
Math Probes	F1	7		148
Math Problem Solving	F2	5		155
Memory Log	T5	5	*	35
Minimal-Advanced Competencies	T1	7	*	19
Mnemonics	T5	3		33
Monitoring Seatwork	G1	20	*	76
Mystery Motivators	I1	3		109
Mystery Motivators	T3	6		27
Note Checks	T10	6	*	57
Note Stacks	T5	4		34
Oral Passage Probes	F1	4		144
Organization Cards	I1	8	*	111

 Quick Reference

TECHNIQUE	QUESTION	NUMBER	REPRODUCIBLE	PAGE #
Overlapping Circles	G3	13	*	85
Pair Interviews	G5	11		103
Parent Partners	I1	12		113
Participation Dots	T3	5	*	26
Participation Jigsaw	T3	3		25
Participation Points	T3	7		27
Partners Plus	I4	9	*	130
Performance Checkouts	F3	3	*	157
Performance Choices	F3	7		159
Performance Conference	F3	2		157
Performance Journal	F3	4		158
Performance Tracking Sheets	F3	1		157
PIRATES	F2	7		156
Plus, Minus, Interesting (PMI)	T7	5		43
Positive and Negative Examples	T7	1		39
Posttest Checklist	F2	4		155
Practice Sheets	I5	11		136
Practice Sheets/Cards	G3	21	*	88
PREPARE	I5	7		134
Presentation Cues	T11	5		61
Processing	G4	8		97
Proofing Skills	I4	4		128
Question Challenge, The	T9	12		54
Reflection Cards	G4	6	*	96
Responsibility Roles	T4	8	*	32
Review Guides	I5	4		133
RIDGES	F2	6		155
Role Cards	G4	5		94
Self-Check and Count	G2	4	*	78
Self-Graphing Charts	I2	8	*	118
Self-Management	I1	11		112
Slice Back	G1	13		73
Slotted Outline	T10	4		56
S.M.A.R.T.S. Review	G5	13	*	104
Social Skill Probes	F1	8	*	149
Split the Assignment	G1	11		72
SQ3R Worksheets	G3	27	*	92

 Quick Reference

TECHNIQUE	QUESTION	NUMBER	REPRODUCIBLE	PAGE #
SR.I.SRV (Scanning)	G3	26	*	91
Star Book Report	G3	15	*	86
Start/Stop Time	G1	19		75
Step-by-Step	G3	12	*	85
Stop and Switch	G2	3		77
Stop and Think	G3	22	*	89
Story Charts	G3	18	*	87
Strategies and Rules	T7	2		41
Students Ask Questions	G3	23	*	90
Study Checklists	I5	5	*	133
Study Guides (Margins)	T7	9		45
Study Guides (Prompts)	G3	24		90
Study Guides (Standard)	T5	6		35
Study Scheduling	I5	3		132
Team-Building Exercises	G4	10		100
Team Skills	G4	4		94
TERM	I5	2		131
Test Study Sheet	I5	1	*	131
Test-Taking Awareness	F2	2		153
Testing Tips	F1	1		141
Think and Write Questions	T11	4	*	60
Time Management Charts	I1	10	*	112
Tracking Directions	T2	9	*	23
Up the Numbers	T9	10		53
What is the Main Idea?	G3	8		83
What, Where/When, and Why Strategy	T6	4	*	37
What Will I Do? Log	T1	6	*	18
Wild Card Spinner	T3	4		25
Word Probes	F1	3	*	143
Write About	I5	8		134
Written Expression Probes	F1	6		147
Yes/No Game	T2	8		23

References

Archer, A. & Gleason, M. (1989). *Skills for school success*. North Billerica, MA: Curriculum Associates.

Beck, R. (1976). *Precision teaching in review, 1973-1976*. Great Falls, MT: Great Falls Public Schools.

Beck, R. (1990). *Project RIDE: Responding to individual differences in education*. Longmont, CO: Sopris West.

Beck, R. (1993). *Project RIDE for preschoolers*. Longmont, CO: Sopris West.

Bellanca, J. & Fogarty, R. (1991). *Blueprints for thinking in the cooperative classroom*. Palantine, IL: IRI/Sky Light.

Bennett, B., Rolheiser-Bennett, C., & Stevahn, L. (1991). *Cooperative learning: Where heart meets mind*. Toronto, Canada: Educational Connections.

Bos, C. & Vaughn, S. (1988). *Strategies for teaching students with learning and behavior problems*. Boston: Allyn and Bacon.

Buchanan, L. (1994, April). *No one is as smart as all of us*. Presentation conducted at International Council for Exceptional Children, Denver.

Carnine, D., Silbert, J., & Kameenui, E. (1990). *Direct instruction reading* (2nd ed.). New York: Macmillian.

DeBoer, A. (1994). *Grading alternatives*. Presentation conducted at Project TIDE Training, Myrtle Beach, South Carolina.

Deshler, D., Schumaker, J., & Nagel, D. (1986). *Learning strategies curriculum: The FIRST strategy*. Lawrence, KS: University of Kansas.

Fister, S.L. & Kemp, K.A. (1994). *Social skills survival kit*. Longmont, CO: Sopris West.

Frost, T. (1987). *TERM: A test preparation strategy for mildly handicapped secondary students*. Unpublished master's thesis, Utah State University, Logan, Utah.

Gable, R., Evans, S., & Evans, W. (1993). It's not over until you examine our answer. *Teaching Exceptional Children*, 25(2), 61-62.

Gibbs, J. (1987). *Tribes: A process for social development and cooperative learning*. Santa Rosa, CA: Center Source Publications.

Greene, L. & Jones-Bamman, L. (1985). *Getting smarter*. Belmont, CA: Lake Publishers.

Howell, K.W., Fox, S.L., & Morehead, M.K. (1993). *Curriculum-based evaluation* (2nd ed.). Pacific Grove, CA: Brooks/Cole Publishing.

Hughes, C.A., Ruhl, K.L., & Peterson, S.K. (1988). Teaching self management skills. *Teaching Exceptional Children*, 20(2), 70-72.

Jenson, W.R., Andrews, D., & Reavis, K. (1993, Fall). Intervention Corner, The "yes" and "no" bag. *The BEST Times*, p. 3.

Jenson, W.R., Rhode, G., & Reavis, H.K. (1994). *The tough kid tool box.* Longmont, CO: Sopris West.

Johnson, D.W., Johnson, R.T., & Bartlett, J.K. (1990). *Cooperative learning lesson structures.* Edina, MN: Interaction Book.

Johnson, R.T., Johnson, D.W., & Holubec, E.J. (Eds.). (1987). *Structuring cooperative learning: Lesson plans for teachers.* Edina, MN: Interaction Book.

Kagan, S. (1990). *Cooperative learning resources for teachers.* Mission Viejo, CA: Resources for Teachers.

Livingston, N. (1991, August). *Reading modifications.* Presentation at Chapter 1 Workshop, Duchesne, UT.

Lovitt, T. (1984). *Tactics for teaching.* Columbus, OH: Merrill.

Lovitt, T., Fister, S., Kemp, K., Moore, R.C., & Schroeder, B.E. (1992). *Translating research into practice (TRIP): Learning strategies.* Longmont, CO: Sopris West.

Lovitt, T., Fister, S., Kemp, K., Moore, R.C., & Schroeder, B.E. (1992). *Translating research into practice (TRIP): Teaching strategies.* Longmont, CO: Sopris West.

Olympia, D., Andrews, D., Valum, L., & Jenson, W. (1993). *Homework teams: Homework management strategies for the classroom.* Longmont, CO: Sopris West.

Pidek, K. (1991). *Assignment notebooks.* Hoffman Estates, IL: Success by Design.

Rhode, G., Jenson, W.R., & Reavis, H.K. (1993). *The tough kid book: Practical classroom management strategies.* Longmont, CO: Sopris West.

Schumaker, J.B., Nolan, S.M., & Deschler, D.D. (1985). *Learning strategies curriculum: The error monitoring strategy.* Lawrence, KS: University of Kansas.

Schumaker, J.B., Deshler, D.D., Alley, G.R., & Warner, M.M. (1983). *Learning strategies curriculum: LINKS strategy.* Lawrence, KS: University of Kansas.

Silbert, J., Carnine, D., & Stein, M. (1990). *Direct instruction mathematics* (2nd ed.). Columbus, OH: Merrill.

Snyder, K. (1987). A problem solving strategy. *Academic Therapy, 23*(2), 261-263.

Sprick, R. (1985). *Discipline in the secondary classroom.* West Nyack, NY: Center for Applied Research.

Starlin, C.M. (1989). *Curriculum based assessment.* Eugene: University of Oregon.

Working Together: The Art of Consulting & Communicating Anita DeBoer

Working Together: The Art of Consulting & Communicating describes how educators can design and engage in peer or collegial problem solving as one way to learn and grow professionally. Based on extensive research, *Working Together: The Art of Consulting & Communicating* addresses the skills educators need when working together: trust-building, listening, facilitating, collaborating, questioning, communicating, and peer problem solving. This is a thoughtful, reader-friendly guide that provides information to allow educators to celebrate their strengths and investigate the ups and downs of collaborative relationships.

Working Together: Tools for Collaborative Teaching Anita DeBoer and Susan Fister

Working Together: Tools for Collaborative Teaching is a hands-on, practical workbook to be used independently or in conjunction with *Working Together: The Art of Consulting & Communicating*. This workbook applies the key principles of peer consulting, presented in its companion piece, through a variety of practical tools that enable educators at grades K-12 to successfully implement collaborative practices in the classroom. Included are: models and structures for collaboration; ideas on how to effectively plan for and schedule collaborative teaching; tips on delivering quality instruction; and techniques for developing systematic methods of evaluating collaborative efforts.

Working Together: What Collaborative Teaching Can Look Like Susan Fister and Anita DeBoer, Developers

Working Together: What Collaborative Teaching Can Look Like is an instructional videotape that can be used independently or in conjunction with the *Working Together* books. The package includes a 24-page manual which highlights and expands on the information presented in the videotape. The program can be used in a variety of ways: as an introduction to collaborative teaching; as a pre-training organizer, training tool, or post-training review; or as part of a complete training program in conjunction with the other *Working Together* materials. At the end of the program, educators will be able to describe collaborative teaching approaches, identify the steps for getting started, discuss ways to apply the model to their setting, and reference additional resources.

TGIF: Making It Work on Monday Susan L. Fister and Karen A. Kemp

TGIF: Making It Work on Monday is a companion to the popular *TGIF: But What Will I Do on Monday?*. Filled with valuable materials for teachers and students, this book of 100 blackline masters includes tracking sheets, organizing forms, handouts, and activity sheets which make the accommodations in *TGIF* easy to implement. Teachers save precious planning time with these ready to use activities and ideas.

For Further Information

Call: (800) 547-6747   or   **Visit Our Website:** www.sopriswest.com